The Flashback Between Us

A Partner's Field Guide to Emotional Flashbacks, Connection, Boundaries, and Repair in CPTSD

Calvin Larkin Tanner

This book is intended as an educational resource. It provides information and ideas about supporting a partner who lives with post-traumatic stress or complex post-traumatic stress. It is not therapy, medical advice, or a treatment protocol, and it is not a substitute for care from a qualified professional. Reading this book does not create a clinical relationship between you and the author. If you or your partner are in crisis, or if anyone is in danger, contact local emergency services or a crisis line in your country.

The response framework described in these pages, including the sequence introduced in Chapter 3, was created by the author as a memory aid for partners. It is not a validated clinical treatment and has not been tested in a trial. A trauma-informed clinician should review any structured approach before a couple relies on it. Treatment of trauma belongs with licensed professionals.

Every case study in this book is a fictional composite. The characters, their circumstances, and their outcomes were constructed to illustrate patterns, not to portray real individuals. Any resemblance to a specific person is coincidental. Names were selected from a fixed, neutral set and carry no information about anyone's background.

First Edition, 2026.

ISBN; 979-8-90678-174-1

State House

Table of Contents

Preface

Research on post-traumatic stress has moved steadily outward from the individual to the relationships that surround them. Studies of couples affected by PTSD and complex PTSD now show what many partners already sense in private, that the condition reaches beyond the person diagnosed and shapes the daily life of the people closest to them. Yet the great majority of trauma resources still speak to the survivor. The partner, who is often the first responder in the room, is left with love, goodwill, and almost no practical instruction.

This book is organized around a single, recurring event: the emotional flashback. An emotional flashback is a sudden return of the feeling state of an old trauma, usually without any accompanying image or clear memory. It is not a picture of the past playing behind the eyes, and it is not ordinary moodiness or a deliberate choice. It is the body reliving a danger it has not finished processing, arriving at full intensity in the present. Naming it precisely matters, because the response that helps a flashback is often the opposite of the response that helps an ordinary bad mood.

The difficulty for most partners is not a lack of care. It is that their instincts, which serve them well in normal conflict, tend to make a flashback worse. Reassurance can register as argument. Questions can land as pressure. Moving closer can feel like threat. Without a framework, a caring partner reaches for the very tools that escalate the moment, then concludes that they are failing at something they were simply never taught.

This book supplies that framework. It follows one flashback from beginning to end, across what happens before, during, and after, and it gives ten plain principles that hold up under stress, along with a simple sequence called PAUSE for the hardest first minute. The aim is practical: to help a partner respond with steadiness rather than panic, to hold boundaries with warmth, to take and offer space without causing injury, and to repair afterward without putting anyone on trial. It also gives honest attention to the cost carried by the supporting partner, whose own steadiness is the resource everything else depends on.

The book stands on its own and assumes no prior reading. It is written first for the spouses and partners of people with PTSD or complex PTSD, and it will also serve family members, close friends, and the clinicians who support couples and want a resource to place in a partner's hands.

A few limits should be clear from the start. This is a guide for the supporting partner, not a treatment manual, and it cannot diagnose a condition or replace the care of a qualified professional. It does not promise to end flashbacks or to repair a relationship on its own, and it treats one question with particular seriousness, the difference between a relationship that is hard and one that is unsafe, without ever asking anyone to remain in danger. What it offers instead is a structured, humane way to stand beside someone in recovery and to remain yourself while you do it.

About the Author

Calvin Larkin Tanner is a researcher who studies how trauma shapes close relationships. He writes practical, warm guides for the people standing beside someone in recovery, in the belief that partners deserve real instruction and not just encouragement. The Flashback Between Us grew out of that conviction.

Introduction

There is a specific kind of fear that does not get talked about much. It is the fear of the person you love changing in front of you, in seconds, into someone you cannot reach. One moment you are folding laundry or planning the week, and the next their face has gone somewhere else. The voice tightens, or drops, or disappears. Their eyes are open but they are not quite looking at you, or they are looking at you as if you are a threat. You reach out and it is wrong. You say something warm and it lands like an attack. You go quiet and that is wrong too. You are standing in your own kitchen with no idea what to do, and the not-knowing is its own kind of panic.

If you have felt that, this book was written for you. Not for your partner, and not for their clinician, though both may find it useful. For you, the person on the other side of the flashback, trying to love someone whose nervous system sometimes reads the present as the past.

You did not sign up to be a therapist, and this book will never ask you to become one. What it will do is give you a place to stand. People who live with complex trauma often describe sudden returns to old feeling-states, waves of fear, shame, or rage that arrive without a clear picture attached (Walker, 2013). When that happens inside a relationship, the partner is usually improvising, and improvising under stress tends to make everyone's worst instincts louder. The research on trauma and relationships is clear that both people feel the strain. Partners of people with post-traumatic stress report more relationship distress and more of their own psychological distress than partners of people without it (Lambert et al., 2012). You are not imagining the weight you are carrying.

Here is the honest promise of this book. It cannot cure your partner, calm every storm, or hand you a script that works every time. Trauma does not run on scripts. What it can do is narrow the problem to something you can actually work with. Instead of trying to understand all of trauma, you will learn to recognize a flashback sooner, steady yourself when one begins, use fewer and better words, hold a limit without cruelty, take space without abandonment, come back together on purpose, and repair afterward in a way that does not require anyone to lose. You will also learn where the line is: the point where a difficult moment stops being a flashback and becomes something that calls for safety, distance, or outside help.

The book is built around one event, the emotional flashback, and it follows that event from before it starts to long after it ends. Each core chapter offers you two views at once. One is a careful, non-diagnostic guess at what may be happening for your partner. The other is what you can safely do from your side of it. You will meet several couples along the way, all of them fictional composites, and you will notice that their stories do not resolve cleanly. That is deliberate. Real support is full of partial wins, clumsy first tries, and nights that go sideways no matter what you do.

One more thing before we begin. Supporting a partner through trauma is voluntary, and it is not the same as being responsible for their recovery. You can be devoted and still have limits. You can love someone and still refuse to stay somewhere unsafe. Holding both of those truths at once is not a contradiction. It is the whole skill. Let us start where the fear starts, in the room, when the past walks in.

Chapter 1: When the Past Enters the Room

Solenne was slicing peppers when the temperature of the kitchen changed. Nothing had happened that she could point to. Auren had been leaning against the counter a moment earlier, telling her about a coworker, and then he was not telling her anything. His sentence had stopped in the middle. When she looked up, his shoulders had climbed toward his ears and his jaw was set in a way she had learned to recognize and still did not understand. She said his name. He did not answer. She said it again, softer, and he flinched as if she had raised her hand.

She was thirty-four years old and had loved this man for six years, and in that instant she had no idea who he was or what he needed. Her first thought was that she had done something. Her second thought was that he was angry at her. Her third thought, the one she hated, was that she wanted to leave the room. All three thoughts were happening while the peppers sat half-cut and Auren, thirty-seven, stood two feet away and somewhere else entirely. This is where most partners live during a flashback. Not in understanding. In the gap before it.

What Solenne was watching had a name, though naming it correctly matters more than naming it fast. People who live with complex post-traumatic stress sometimes drop, without warning, into the emotional weather of an old and unsafe time. The therapist Pete Walker called these emotional flashbacks and described them as sudden regressions into overwhelming feeling-states from the past, often without any picture or memory attached to explain them (Walker, 2013). That last part is what makes them so confusing to witness. There is frequently no scene playing behind your partner's eyes, nothing they could describe if you asked. There is only the feeling, arriving at full volume, as if the danger were now. Researchers have proposed that trauma can be stored in a fragmented, sensory form that returns as raw emotion and body sensation rather than as an ordered narrative, which helps explain why a flashback can carry so much feeling and so little story (Brewin et al., 1996).

What a flashback is, and what it is not

It helps to be precise about the thing we are talking about, because precision is protective. A flashback is not your partner deciding to shut you out. It is not manipulation, and it is not a verdict on your relationship. In the clinical language of the World Health Organization's diagnostic system, complex post-traumatic stress includes the core features of post-traumatic stress, re-experiencing, avoidance, and a persistent sense of current threat, along with lasting difficulties in three further areas: managing emotions, holding a steady sense of self, and staying close to other people (Cloitre et al., 2018). An emotional flashback sits at the intersection of the sense of current threat and the difficulty managing emotion. The body has concluded, faster than thought, that it is in danger, and it has begun to run an old program.

That old program was not chosen. Trauma researchers describe how, under threat, the parts of the brain that handle fast danger-detection can fire ahead of the parts that reason and put words to experience (LeDoux, 1996). Your partner is not being unreasonable in a moment like this because reason is temporarily not the system in charge. Understanding that one fact changes how you hold everything else. You are not in an argument that logic can win. You are in a moment where someone's alarm has gone off, and the alarm does not care that the house is not actually on fire.

There is a second precision that matters just as much, and it points the other way. Not every hard moment is a flashback. Sometimes your partner is simply tired, or irritated, or disagreeing with you for ordinary reasons that have nothing to do with trauma. Sometimes they are wrong and you are right and the two of you are just having a conflict, the kind every couple has. The danger of learning about flashbacks is that you can start seeing them everywhere, filing every frown and every silence under the same heading. That is its own mistake, and we will come back to it, because it can quietly rob your partner of being an ordinary person having ordinary feelings.

Why partners reach for a diagnosis

When you are frightened and confused, the mind wants an answer, and it wants it now. So partners tend to grab the nearest explanation and hold on. He is angry at me. She is punishing me. They are being dramatic. He is doing this on purpose. Each of these is a diagnosis, and each of them feels like relief for about a second because at least it is something to know. The trouble is that these fast diagnoses are usually wrong, and acting on a wrong diagnosis is how a difficult moment becomes a damaging one.

Consider Vaelan, twenty-nine, who spent the first year of their relationship convinced that their partner's sudden withdrawals were a sign of fading love. Every time their partner went flat and far away, Vaelan read it as rejection and responded by pursuing, questioning, pushing for reassurance. It made a terrible kind of sense from the inside. It also made every episode longer and worse, because a person whose alarm is already screaming does not have room for someone demanding to know whether they are still loved. Vaelan was not cruel. Vaelan was frightened and reaching for the only explanation that fit their fear. The explanation was wrong, and being wrong cost them both.

This is the first thing this book will ask you to hold, and it is harder than it sounds.

The Uncertain Witness

You can respond well to something you do not fully understand. In fact, you almost always have to. The principle that will carry you through this entire book is what I will call the Uncertain Witness: your job in the moment is not to diagnose what is happening inside your partner, it is to respond to what you can actually see while leaving the interpretation open. You are a witness, not a judge, and a good witness reports rather than concludes.

Being an uncertain witness sounds passive. It is the opposite. It takes real discipline to stand in a charged moment and not seize the first story that would explain it. Solenne, in her kitchen, had three stories ready, and each one would have led her to act, to apologize, to defend herself, to leave. The skill she was about to learn was to notice all three stories, set them down, and stay with what was in front of her: a person she loved whose body had gone into alarm. She did not need to know why. She needed to know that something had shifted, and that pushing would not help.

The language you use inside your own head is part of this. There is a large difference between thinking he is attacking me and thinking something has changed for him. The first is a conclusion that will shape your next move toward defense. The second is an observation that keeps your options open. Trauma clinicians who work with couples emphasize how much the partner's private interpretation of a symptom drives what happens next, for better or worse (Renshaw et al., 2008). You cannot always control the feeling that rises in you. You can, with practice, control the sentence you tell yourself about it.

Why this protects both of you

Refusing to diagnose is not only kind to your partner. It protects you, because most of the fast diagnoses partners reach for are self-blaming or self-endangering, and neither serves you. When Solenne assumed she had caused the shift, she loaded herself with a responsibility that was not hers to carry. When Vaelan assumed rejection, they signed up for a nightly referendum on whether they were still wanted. The Uncertain Witness sets that weight down. You do not have to decide, in the middle of a hard moment, whose fault it is or what it means. You get to wait for information.

It also keeps you honest about the times when something really is wrong. If you have trained yourself to observe rather than conclude, you are far better positioned to notice the difference between a flashback and a genuine threat, which is the subject of the final chapter of this book. A partner who labels everything a flashback is as blind as a partner who labels nothing one. Both have stopped watching and started assuming. The whole point of witnessing is that you keep your eyes open, and open eyes see the exceptions.

None of this means you become a passive observer of your own relationship. There is a great deal you can do, and the chapters ahead are full of it. But all of it rests on this foundation. Before you can respond well, you have to resist the pull to explain too soon. The research on trauma and intimate relationships shows how easily these moments spiral into conflict and distance when both people are running on assumption (Taft et al., 2011). The Uncertain Witness is how you step out of the spiral before it starts.

A note on the two views

Throughout this book you will find two perspectives side by side. One is a careful, tentative account of what may be happening for your partner. The other is what you can actually do from where you stand. I keep these separate on purpose, because collapsing them is how partners get into trouble. You are not inside your partner's experience and you cannot be. You can make a humble guess about it, and you can act cleanly on your own side. Notice the words in the guessing column. May. Could. Perhaps. Might. Those words are not hedging. They are accuracy. Anyone who tells you exactly what is happening inside another person's nervous system is selling certainty that no one actually has.

For your side, the words are different. Slow down. Lower your voice. Ask less. Offer a choice. Stay near or step back. These are things you can do without knowing the inner story, and they tend to help across a wide range of inner stories. That is why they are worth practicing. A response that only works if your guess is correct is fragile. A response that helps whether or not you understand the cause is sturdy, and sturdy is what you want when the ground is moving.

Two views of the same moment

Because this device runs through the whole book, let me show you both panels fully for the moment Solenne faced, so the shape is clear before we build on it. Read them as two separate columns of attention, one turned toward your partner and one turned toward your own next move, and notice that you can act well on the second without being certain about the first.

What may be happening for your partner. Something in the room, a tone, a word, a gesture, a smell, may have matched an old danger closely enough to trip the alarm, often below the level of anything they could name. They may be flooded with fear, shame, or rage that has no picture attached, which can make the feeling even more disorienting for them than for you. Their capacity for language and reason may have narrowed, so that your words are reaching a system that cannot fully process them. They are very likely not thinking about you at all in the way you fear, because in that state there is rarely room for anything but the alarm itself. And when it passes, they may feel exposed, ashamed, or afraid that they have damaged something, which shapes how you will want to come back together later.

What you can safely do from your side. You can slow your own body first, because a calm presence nearby is something you can offer regardless of what is happening inside them. You can resist the pull to explain, defend, or diagnose, and instead simply stay, present and unhurried, without insisting on understanding. You can keep your private interpretation open, choosing something has shifted over he is attacking me, so that your next move comes from observation rather than from a fast, frightened conclusion. You can wait, giving the moment room rather than forcing it toward resolution. And you can hold the knowledge that this will pass, which it almost always does, so that your own alarm does not convince you that the current state is permanent.

Notice again the words in the first panel, may and often and very likely, against the plain verbs in the second, slow and stay and wait. That contrast is not stylistic. It is the difference between what you can only guess at and what you can actually do, and keeping them separate is the whole discipline of the uncertain witness.

This week

Here is one thing to try before the next chapter, and it asks nothing of your partner. For the next several days, when you notice a shift in them, any shift, catch the first sentence that appears in your mind. Just catch it. You do not have to change it or act on it. Write it down later if that helps. You are looking for your own reflexive diagnoses, the stories your fear reaches for. Most people find they have two or three that repeat. Once you can see yours, you have already begun to loosen their grip, because a story you can name is a story you can question. That is the entire practice of the Uncertain Witness, and everything else in this book is built on top of it.

A question partners ask

Partners often ask how they are supposed to tell a flashback from ordinary moodiness in the moment, and the honest answer is that you frequently cannot, and do not need to. The uncertain witness does not depend on correct identification. The moves you will learn, slowing down, using fewer words, offering a choice, tend to help across both a flashback and an ordinary bad mood, which is exactly why they are worth building. You are not running a diagnostic test whose result determines your response. You are offering a steady, low-pressure presence that is useful whether the cause is old trauma or a hard day at work. Over weeks and months, and mostly in calm conversations rather than heated ones, you will learn your particular partner's patterns well enough to guess more often than not. But the entire point of this first principle is that your response does not hinge on the guess. Free yourself from needing to know, and you will act better than the partner who is certain and wrong.

Back in the Room

Return to Solenne for a moment, because her kitchen is where this chapter began and it is where the work actually lives. She did not solve anything that evening. She set down the knife, she stopped saying his name, and she stood a little apart, present but not pushing, while Auren slowly came back into himself over the next several minutes. It was clumsy. She felt useless the whole time. Later she would learn there were better things she could have done, and you will learn them too. But that night she did the one thing that mattered most, which was to not make it worse by insisting she already knew what it was. She stayed an uncertain witness in a room where the past had briefly walked in, and she let it walk back out without turning it into a war. In the next chapter, we move earlier, to the minutes and signals before the past arrives at all.

Chapter 2: Learn Your Partner's Early Signals

You already collect data on your partner. You know their tells better than you think. You know the difference between the quiet that means they are content and the quiet that means something is wrong. You know which sigh is tiredness and which sigh is the beginning of a bad evening. You have been reading this person for years, gathering a private catalog of their small changes, and most of the time you do not even know you are doing it. The problem is not that you lack information. The problem is that you have never organized it, checked it, or shared it with the one person who could confirm whether you are reading it right.

That is what this chapter is about. Not becoming a more anxious observer, watching your partner for cracks. The opposite. Turning the watching you already do into something clearer, calmer, and agreed upon, so that you spend less energy scanning and more energy responding well when it counts. The goal is to see the early signals of a flashback sooner, and to see them together, out loud, in a conversation you both chose to have.

Why the middle is too late

By the time a flashback is in full force, your options have narrowed to a handful of gentle, damage-limiting moves. Earlier, when your partner is just beginning to leave the window in which they can stay present and connected, there is more room. Clinicians describe a window of tolerance, a zone of arousal within which a person can feel their feelings and still think, still relate, still stay in the room (Siegel, 1999). Above that window is a flooded, revved-up state. Below it is a shut-down, numb, faraway state. Both are ways of leaving the window, and both have early signs.

The early signs are quieter than the flashback itself, which is exactly why they are useful. A voice that tightens by half a degree. A slightly longer pause before answering. Eyes that start to track the exits, or eyes that stop tracking anything. A hand that moves to the back of the neck. Feet that turn toward the door. Body-oriented trauma therapists have long paid attention to these small shifts because the body often signals a change in state before the mind can name it (Ogden et al., 2006). You do not need to become an expert in any of this. You need to learn your specific partner's specific early signs, the two or three that reliably show up before things get hard.

The Consent Map

Here is the principle that keeps this from going wrong. A signal map only helps if you built it together, in calm, with consent. Call it the Consent Map. You do not get to decide, on your own, what your partner's signals mean and then start narrating them back to them mid-episode. That is not support. That is surveillance, and it tends to make a person feel watched, managed, and reduced to their symptoms. The map has to be a shared document, made when you are both settled, that your partner has helped write and agreed to.

The difference matters more than it might seem. A partner who quietly tracks every micro-expression and then announces I can tell you are getting triggered has taken something that should belong to the couple and made it a one-sided assessment. Trauma researchers studying couples have found that partners can slide into patterns of accommodation and control that feel like help but corrode the relationship over time (Fredman et al., 2014). The Consent Map is the antidote. Because your partner helped build it, the signals are theirs as much as yours, and pointing to one becomes a shared reference rather than a diagnosis imposed from outside.

How Novaire and Isoren built theirs

Novaire, forty-six, had spent two years feeling ambushed. Her partner Isoren, forty-eight, would seem fine and then not fine, and she never saw the turn. She described it as being on a boat that lurched without warning. What finally helped was not watching him harder. It was sitting down with him on a calm Sunday, with no episode anywhere near them, and asking a question she had never asked directly: when you start to go under, what happens first that you actually notice?

Isoren surprised her. He said that before anything showed on the outside, he felt a specific coldness in his hands, and a sense that sounds were getting sharper. Novaire had never known that, because it was invisible to her. In return, she told him what she saw from the outside, that his answers got shorter and he stopped making eye contact. Neither of them had the full picture alone. Together, over that one conversation, they built a short, plain list: his internal early sign, her external early sign, and one thing he said he wanted her to do when either appeared, which was simply to stop asking questions. It was not elaborate. It fit on an index card. It changed the next several months.

Not every attempt goes that smoothly, and it is worth saying so. Isoren could not always feel the coldness in his hands before he was already gone. Sometimes there was no runway at all, and the map was useless because the flashback arrived at full speed. That is normal. A map reduces surprises. It does not eliminate them, and a partner who expects it to will end up disappointed and blaming. The map is a tool that works often, not a system that works always.

What goes on the map

When you build yours, keep it small and concrete. Six domains are worth asking about, and you do not need all of them. Voice: does it get quieter, tighter, flatter, louder. Distance: does your partner move closer or pull away, physically or emotionally. Movement: do they get restless, or go still, or start doing something repetitive with their hands. Attention: do they lock onto something, or scatter, or seem to look through you. Touch: does contact suddenly help or suddenly hurt, and does the answer change. Communication: do sentences get shorter, do they stop, does the tone change from the words. Ask your partner which of these ring true, and add the internal signs only they can report.

The most valuable line on the map is not a signal at all. It is the one thing your partner tells you they want when a signal appears. This is the part partners most often get wrong by guessing. What helps one person feels invasive to another. Some people want you to move closer. Some need you to move back. Some want you to say a specific short phrase. Some want silence. You cannot deduce this. You have to ask, in calm, and then believe the answer even when it contradicts your instinct to comfort. Éloane, thirty-nine, told her partner Cyrel exactly this in one of their early conversations, and it saved them a great deal of grief later, which we will see.

When you cannot ask directly

Some partners cannot yet talk about their signals. The topic is too raw, or they do not have the words, or being asked feels like being studied. If that is where you are, do not force the conversation. You can still build a private, provisional version of the map for yourself, held loosely, treated as a hypothesis rather than fact. The difference from surveillance is honesty about its status. You are not deciding what is true about your partner. You are noticing patterns and staying ready to be wrong, and you are leaving the door open for a real conversation when they are ready to have one.

You can also lower the stakes of the conversation by making it mutual. You have early signals too. When you get frightened or overwhelmed, your voice and body change in ways your partner might learn to read. Offering your own signals first turns the map from something done to your partner into something you are building together as equals. It is a small reframe and it changes the temperature of the whole discussion. The person with trauma is used to being the subject of concern. Being asked to help you, in return, can be a relief.

Watching without hovering

There is a failure mode to name before we move on, because it catches thoughtful, loving partners most of all. Once you start watching for early signals, it is easy to watch too much. You can turn every dinner into a monitoring session, scanning your partner's face for the first sign of trouble, so anxious about the next episode that your anxiety becomes its own pressure in the room. Your partner feels it. Being perpetually observed is not restful for anyone, and for someone whose nervous system is already braced for threat, it can make the very state you are trying to prevent more likely.

The Consent Map is meant to reduce your watching, not increase it. Once you and your partner both know the two or three signals that matter, you can let the rest go. You do not have to catalog every mood. You are waiting for a small number of agreed signs, and the rest of the time you get to just be with the person you love. If you notice yourself scanning constantly, treat that as information about your own state, not theirs. It usually means you are frightened, and your fear deserves care of its own, which is the subject of a later chapter. For now, notice it, breathe, and return your attention to the ordinary evening in front of you.

Two views of the early signals

The mirrored panels are useful here too, because early signals look different from the inside than from the outside, and the map you build together lives in the gap between the two views.

What may be happening for your partner. As they begin to leave their window of tolerance, they may feel an internal shift long before anything shows on the surface, a change in temperature, a sharpening of sound, a tightening in the chest, a sense of the room getting smaller. They may not have words for it in the moment, and they may not even recognize it as the beginning of a hard time until it is well underway. Being watched for signs of trouble may feel intrusive to them, like being studied or reduced to their symptoms, especially if the watching is one-sided. They may also want very different things than you would guess, so that the comfort you instinctively offer is exactly what they need less of. And they may find it a relief, rather than a burden, to be asked directly and calmly what they notice first, because it hands the expertise about their own experience back to them.

What you can safely do from your side. You can learn the two or three external signs that reliably precede a hard moment, the shorter answers, the turned shoulders, the dropped eye contact, and hold them lightly as patterns rather than certainties. You can build the map together, in calm, so that pointing to a signal later is a shared reference rather than a verdict. You can ask, once, in a settled moment, what your partner notices first, and then believe their answer even when it contradicts your instinct. You can offer your own early signals in return, making the map mutual rather than a study of them. And you can let the rest go, watching for only the few agreed signs instead of scanning constantly, so that most of the time you are simply with the person you love rather than monitoring them.

The whole value of the two panels here is that they keep you from filling your partner's inner column with your own guesses. You supply the outer view. They supply the inner one. The map is what happens when you stop guessing across that gap and start asking across it instead.

This week

The application here is a conversation, and the timing is the whole point. Do not have it during or right after a hard moment. Wait for a genuinely calm stretch, a walk, a quiet drive, a slow morning, and ask one open question: when things start to get hard for you, is there anything you notice first, before it gets bad? Then listen without fixing. If your partner offers something, thank them and add nothing. If they cannot yet, let it go and offer your own signals instead, so the door stays open. One question, asked in calm, is the entire assignment. You are not building the whole map this week. You are starting the kind of conversation the map is made of.

A question partners ask

A common worry is what to do when your partner refuses to talk about their signals at all, treating the whole subject as intrusive or off limits.

Push, and you confirm that the topic is a threat. So do not push. You can hold a loose, private, provisional set of observations, clearly labeled in your own mind as guesses rather than facts, and you can leave a standing, gentle invitation open without forcing it through. You can also lower the temperature by offering your own signals first and asking your partner only to help you, which flips the usual dynamic in which they are always the subject of concern. Some partners come to the conversation months after it is first offered, once they have watched you handle their hard moments without weaponizing what you learn. Trust, here, is earned by what you do during flashbacks, not by what you say between them. A partner who has seen you stay calm and non-diagnostic is far more likely to eventually help build the map than one who has only been asked to.

What the Map Is For

It is worth being clear about what a signal map can and cannot do, because partners tend to overload it with hope. A map cannot prevent flashbacks. It cannot make your partner's trauma smaller or their recovery faster. It cannot guarantee you will always see the turn coming, because sometimes there is no turn to see. What it can do is buy you time and lower your panic. When a signal you both recognize appears, you are no longer improvising from fear. You have a shared reference and a plan you agreed on together, which means you can move earlier and more gently, before the window closes all the way. That is the entire value, and it is considerable. A few extra seconds of calm at the start of a hard moment can change everything that follows. Those seconds are not trivial. They are often the whole difference between a moment that settles and one that spirals, and the map is how you buy them. It will not work every time, and the times it fails are not evidence that you did it wrong. It is a tool that tilts the odds, and tilting the odds, night after night, adds up to a relationship that feels less like an ambush and more like something the two of you are facing together. The next chapter is about what to do with those seconds.

Chapter 3: The First Response

There is a belief that quietly runs most partners' behavior in a crisis, and it is wrong. The belief is that when your partner is in distress, you are supposed to do something active about it. Talk them down. Reason them out of it. Find the right words, the magic combination that dissolves the fear. Fix it. This belief feels responsible and loving, which is why it is so hard to see as a mistake. But in the first moments of an emotional flashback, doing more is usually doing harm, and the skilled response looks, from the outside, almost like doing nothing at all.

Understanding why requires a short look at what is actually happening in those first moments. When the brain registers threat, whether the threat is real or an echo of an old one, fast survival circuitry can take over before the reasoning, language-using parts of the mind come back online (LeDoux, 1996). Your partner in a flashback is not choosing to be unreachable by reason. Reason is temporarily offstage. This is why the well-meant explanation, the you are safe, the nothing is wrong, the let me explain why this is fine, tends to bounce off or make things worse. You are offering logic to a system that has, for the moment, stopped running on logic.

The myth of talking it out

The myth of talking it out is stubborn because in ordinary conflict, talking it out is exactly right. Most relationship advice, most of the time, points toward more communication, more expression, more working through it together. Those instincts are good, and this book is not against them. But a flashback is not ordinary conflict, and importing conflict tools into it is like bringing a hammer to a task that needs a feather. Trauma researchers describe how re-experiencing carries a sense of nowness, the past felt as present threat rather than remembered as past (Ehlers & Clark, 2000). A flood of words, however kind, adds input to a system that is already overwhelmed by input. Less reaches the person than you think, and what does reach them is often just the pressure of your urgency.

Solenne learned this the hard way in the weeks after the evening in the kitchen. Having read a little about trauma, she overcorrected. The next time Auren went far away, she moved in close and started talking, a steady stream of reassurance, it is okay, I am here, you are safe, nothing bad is happening. She meant every word. Auren's shoulders climbed higher. His breathing got shorter. Her reassurance, delivered as a wall of sound at close range, was landing on his nervous system as more, not less. She was doing everything her love told her to do, and it was not working, and she could not understand why.

The Half-Speed Rule

What Solenne eventually learned is the principle at the center of this chapter. In the first moments of a flashback, cut everything in half. Half the words, half the volume, half the movement, half the speed. Call it the Half-Speed Rule. Your instinct under stress is to speed up, to move toward, to fill the silence, to make something happen. The skill is to deliberately do the reverse. Slow your own body first, because your partner's nervous system is reading yours, and a calm body nearby is a signal of safety that no sentence can match (van der Kolk, 2014).

This is genuinely counterintuitive, and it will feel wrong the first several times. Slowing down while someone you love is suffering feels like abandonment or passivity. It is neither. You are not withdrawing your care. You are changing the form your care takes, from active intervention to steady, unhurried presence. A person leaving their window of tolerance does not need you to reach in and pull them out by force. They need the room to feel a little safer, and the fastest way to make a room feel safer is to be the calmest, slowest thing in it (Siegel, 1999).

The Half-Speed Rule starts with you, not them. Before you do anything toward your partner, do something for your own body. Drop your shoulders. Unclench your jaw. Let your next breath out slowly, longer on the exhale than the inhale. This is not a spa technique. It is the practical first move, because you cannot offer a regulated presence from a dysregulated body, and your partner will feel the difference in seconds. Everything else in this chapter depends on you doing this one thing first.

A sequence you can hold onto

When people are frightened, they cannot hold complicated instructions. That is true of your partner in a flashback, and it is true of you in the moment you are trying to help. So I want to give you something small enough to remember when your own heart is pounding. I created a five-step sequence as a memory aid for partners, and I want to be plain about what it is and is not. It is not a validated treatment. It has not been tested in a trial. It is a way to organize what this book teaches so you can find it under stress. If you and your partner want to lean on it, have a trauma-informed clinician look it over first, and adjust it to fit your specific relationship.

The sequence spells PAUSE, which is also the instruction. P is Pause: stop what you are doing and slow your own body before you do anything toward your partner. A is Assess safety: take one clear look at whether anyone is in physical danger, which almost always they are not, but the check matters and we return to it in the final chapter. U is Use fewer words: switch from explaining to the smallest, calmest language possible, or to none. S is Support choice: instead of directing your partner, offer them a small, concrete option that hands a little control back. E is Exit or reconnect: read whether this moment needs space or nearness, and follow that rather than your default.

Each of those steps gets a chapter or a section of its own later in the book, so you do not need to master them now. What matters here is the shape. Pause first. Check safety. Shrink your words. Offer a choice. Then either give space or move closer, depending on what this moment and this person actually need. Notice that four of the five steps are about doing less or doing smaller. That is the whole spirit of the first response.

Support choice, not compliance

Of the five steps, the one partners find most surprising is supporting choice. When someone is flooded, a natural instinct is to take charge, to tell them what to do, to become the calm authority issuing instructions. Sit down. Breathe. Look at me. Drink this. The intention is good and the effect is often bad, because a person whose alarm is about powerlessness experiences a stream of commands as more of the thing they cannot bear. Trauma very often involves the loss of control, and moments that restore even a small amount of choice tend to help (Herman, 1992).

So instead of directing, offer. The grammar is small but it matters. Not sit down, but would sitting help, or would you rather stand. Not drink this, but there is water here if you want it. Not tell me what is wrong, but I am here whether you want to talk or not. Each of these hands your partner a choice they can accept or decline, and the choosing itself is part of the medicine. You are not solving the flashback. You are quietly returning agency to someone who has temporarily lost the feeling of having any.

What Solenne did differently

The next time it happened, months after the kitchen, Solenne caught herself before the wall of words. She felt the old urgency rise, the pull to move in and fix, and she recognized it. She let out one slow breath. She did not close the distance. She lowered herself into a chair a few feet away, which put her below Auren's eye level and slowed the whole scene down. She said one short sentence, quietly: I am here, no rush. Then she stopped talking. It cost her enormous effort to stop talking.

It was not a clean success. Auren stayed gone for several more minutes, and Solenne sat in the discomfort of not-doing, second-guessing herself the entire time. But the episode did not escalate the way the reassurance-flood had. He came back slightly sooner, and when he did, he was able to say, roughly, that the talking usually made it worse and the quiet had helped. That was the first time either of them had a piece of real information about what worked, and they only got it because Solenne did less. The Half-Speed Rule did not fix Auren's trauma. It kept a hard moment from becoming a harder one, and it produced knowledge they could use next time.

When your own alarm goes off

There is a version of this you need to prepare for, because it is common and rarely discussed. Sometimes, watching your partner go into a flashback trips your own alarm. Their fear becomes your fear. Your heart races, your thoughts scramble, and you find you cannot slow anything because you are not calm either. This does not make you a bad partner. It makes you a human being whose nervous system is also wired for threat, and it is worth knowing that partners of people with post-traumatic stress can develop their own trauma-related responses over time (National Center for PTSD, n.d.-a).

When this happens, the Half-Speed Rule still applies, but the first person you are slowing is yourself, and sometimes the honest move is to get a small amount of distance so you can regulate before you try to help. Stepping into the next room to take three slow breaths is not desertion. A partner who floods alongside their partner and then tries to help from that flooded state usually makes the moment worse for both of them. Taking care of your own alarm first is not selfish. It is what makes you useful, and it is the beginning of a much larger theme in this book about protecting the person who does the supporting.

Two views of the first minute

The first minute of a flashback is where the two panels matter most, because it is the minute in which partners do the most damage by acting on the wrong view. Here is each side laid out.

What may be happening for your partner. Their fast survival circuitry may have taken over, so that reason and language are temporarily not the systems in charge. They may be experiencing the past as present, a sense of nowness that makes your reassurances about safety feel like arguments against their own reality. They may be flooded to the point where additional input, even loving input, registers mostly as pressure rather than comfort. They may have lost, in that moment, the feeling of having any control, which is often the very core of what the old trauma was about. And their body may be reading your body, so that your urgency, your fast movements, and your raised voice may be adding to the alarm without a single word being exchanged.

What you can safely do from your side. You can pause and slow your own body before you do anything toward them, because you cannot offer a regulated presence from a dysregulated one. You can check, quickly and quietly, whether anyone is actually in physical danger, which almost always they are not. You can shrink your words to the smallest, calmest possible, or to none, matching your language to what they can actually receive. You can offer a small choice rather than issuing a command, handing back a little of the control the moment has taken. And you can read whether this particular moment needs nearness or space, and follow that reading rather than your default habit. Four of those five moves are about doing less, and that is the point.

If you hold these two panels together, the counterintuitive shape of the first response stops feeling like doing nothing and starts feeling like doing the right thing. You are not passive. You are matching your action to a situation that punishes force and rewards steadiness, and you are letting the humble words in the first panel keep you from overconfident action in the second.

This week

The practice this week is a behavior, and you can rehearse it before you ever need it. Pick the physical reset you will use, the one that slows your own body, and practice it when nothing is wrong. It might be the long exhale, or dropping your shoulders, or pressing your feet into the floor. Do it a few times a day in calm moments, so that it becomes something your body knows how to find without thinking. You are building muscle memory for the Pause, the first letter and the first move, so that when the real moment comes, your body has somewhere to go before your fear takes the wheel.

A question partners ask

Partners often ask whether the Half-Speed Rule means they should never touch, never move, never do anything at all, and the answer is no, it means you do less and you do it slower, guided by what your partner has told you helps. Some people, in some moments, want a hand held or an arm around them, and if your partner has said so in calm, then offering that, gently and without insisting, is part of the response, not a violation of it. The rule is about removing your reflexive urgency, not about becoming a statue. What you are cutting in half is the frantic, fixing, filling energy that stress pulls out of you, not your warmth or your responsiveness. A slow, offered touch is very different from a fast, imposed one, and the difference is exactly the difference the rule is pointing at. Slow does not mean absent. It means deliberate, unhurried, and shaped by your partner's stated preferences rather than by your own need to be doing something.

The Minute Before the Words

Almost everything in this chapter happens before anyone says much of anything. The pause, the slowed body, the shrinking of words, the offered choice, these are the work of the first minute, and they mostly precede language. But eventually, in most flashbacks, there is something to say. A few words do get exchanged, and which words you choose matters enormously, because the wrong ones can undo a minute of careful calm in a single sentence. Having learned to slow down and use fewer words, the question becomes which fewer words. That is where we go next, into the small, careful language that reduces pressure instead of adding it.

Chapter 4: Words That Reduce Pressure

"Just tell me what I did." Lorien had said it a hundred times, in a hundred slightly different shapes, and it had never once helped. She was thirty-one and exhausted by her own good intentions. When her partner Zevian, thirty-three, dropped into that shut-down, faraway state, her whole body strained toward understanding, and understanding, to her, meant asking. What happened? What did I do? What are you feeling? Why won't you talk to me? Each question was an act of love and each one landed on Zevian like a hand pressing on a bruise. He did not have answers. He barely had words. And every question she asked was a demand for words he did not have.

This chapter is about the small number of words worth saying in a flashback, and the larger number worth not saying. In the last chapter you learned to use fewer words. Here we get specific about which ones, because the difference between a sentence that reduces pressure and a sentence that adds it can be a single word, and in a charged moment single words carry a great deal of weight.

Four kinds of sentence that make it worse

It helps to know your enemy, and the enemy here is four familiar, well-meant categories of speech. The first is reassurance delivered as fact: you are safe, nothing is wrong, everything is fine. It fails because it argues with your partner's felt experience. Their body is reporting danger, and being told there is no danger can feel like being told they are wrong about their own reality, which adds shame to fear. The second is interrogation: the string of questions Lorien specialized in. Questions demand cognitive work, retrieval, and language, exactly the capacities that go offline in a flashback (Ehlers & Clark, 2000). Even gentle questions are, in that moment, a workload.

The third is correction: no, that's not what happened, you're overreacting, this isn't a big deal. Correction treats a flashback as a factual dispute to be won, and it cannot be won, because the issue was never the facts. The fourth is forced discussion: we need to talk about this right now, I can't just leave it, tell me what's going on. Forced discussion insists on processing at the exact moment when processing is impossible. All four come from love. All four increase pressure. Naming them is the first step to catching yourself before they leave your mouth.

The Smaller Sentence

The principle to hold is this. In a flashback, the shorter and simpler your sentence, the more of it your partner can actually receive. Call it the Smaller Sentence. A long, complex, emotionally loaded statement is mostly noise to a flooded nervous system. A short, plain, low-demand sentence can get through. This is not about being cold or withholding. It is about matching your language to your partner's actual capacity in the moment, which is a form of respect, not distance.

The best in-the-moment sentences share a few features. They are short. They make no demand. They offer presence or a choice rather than requiring an answer. And they leave your partner free to respond or not. I am here. Take your time. No rush. I am not going anywhere. There is water if you want it. We do not have to talk. Each of these can be said quietly, in a handful of words, and none of them requires your partner to produce anything. That last quality is the key. A sentence that requires a response is a demand. A sentence that offers something and asks for nothing is a gift.

Trading questions for offers

Since interrogation is the trap thoughtful partners fall into most, it is worth building the specific habit of turning questions into offers. This is the small series I recommend practicing, because it converts your loving instinct into a form your partner can use. When you feel the urge to ask what's wrong, offer instead: I am here whether or not you want to talk.

When you want to ask what did I do, offer: we can figure anything out later, there is no rush now. When you want to ask are you okay, which demands an assessment your partner cannot make, offer: I am right here. When you want to demand tell me what you need, which asks a flooded person to know and articulate their needs, offer two concrete choices instead: would it help if I stayed close, or would it help if I gave you some room?

That last one deserves emphasis because it does double duty. It uses fewer words, and it supports choice, which you met in the last chapter. It also gathers information without interrogating, because whichever your partner chooses tells you something real about what they need, and they only had to pick between two options rather than generate an answer from nothing. Over time, these offered choices teach you your partner's patterns more reliably than any amount of questioning, and they do it without adding load.

Consent lives in the language

There is a quiet form of consent built into good flashback language, and it is worth making visible. When you say we do not have to talk, you are handing your partner permission to be silent. When you say there is water if you want it, you are handing them permission to decline. When you say I can stay or give you space, whatever you want, you are handing them authority over the distance between you. Each of these sentences respects that your partner, even flooded, gets to have a say in what happens to and around them. Given that trauma so often involves having no say, this matters more than its small size suggests (Herman, 1992).

Contrast that with the commanding language that stress pulls out of us. Sit down. Breathe. Calm down. Look at me. Even said with love, these remove choice, and calm down in particular has never once in human history helped anyone calm down. The consent-based version is always available and almost always better. Rather than breathe, you can say I am going to slow my breathing down, want to do it with me, which invites without commanding. Rather than look at me, you can simply stay in view and let your partner find your face when they are ready. The instruction becomes an invitation, and the invitation carries no threat.

When words are not the tool at all

Sometimes the most pressure-reducing thing you can offer is not a sentence but silence, and it is important to say clearly that silence is a legitimate response, not a failure. If your partner has told you, in calm, that they want quiet during a hard moment, then giving them quiet is doing the work, even though it feels like doing nothing. A calm, unhurried body a few feet away, saying almost nothing, communicates safety in a language older than words (van der Kolk, 2014). You do not have to fill the air. You have to be a steady presence in it.

This is hard for partners who equate love with active helping, and there is no shame in finding silence excruciating. The discomfort is yours to manage, and managing it is part of the skill. If you cannot bear to say nothing, choose one very short anchoring sentence and repeat it sparingly rather than adding new content. I am here is enough for a whole episode. You do not need variety. You need to be a fixed point, and a fixed point does not keep talking. The urge to say more is usually your anxiety asking to be soothed, not your partner asking for more words.

Lorien and the one question

Lorien did not become a different person overnight. Trading her questions for offers went against a lifetime of instinct, and she failed at it often. What shifted things was a single conversation with Zevian on a calm evening, when she asked him, genuinely, which of her questions was the worst. He told her it was why won't you talk to me, because it made him feel that his silence was hurting her, which piled guilt on top of everything else. That one piece of information let her retire that one sentence, and retiring it changed the tone of their hard moments more than any technique she had tried.

She still slipped. There were nights she peppered him with questions before she caught herself, and nights the offers came out stiff and rehearsed. But she had traded her single most damaging sentence for silence, and even that partial change lowered the pressure in the room. Meanwhile Solenne, whom you have been following, was learning the same lesson from the other direction. Having stopped flooding Auren with reassurance, she discovered that her three-word sentence, I am here, no rush, worked better the fewer times she said it. Both women were learning that in this domain, less language is more love, and that the hardest word to master is the one you do not say.

A caution about scripts

I have given you specific sentences, and I want to warn you against using them like a script. A memorized phrase delivered mechanically, in the wrong tone, at the wrong moment, can feel to your partner like being handed a customer-service line. These sentences are starting points, meant to be shaped to your relationship and your partner's actual preferences, which you learn by asking in calm. The words matter, but the tone and timing matter more, and no list can teach those. Trauma-focused couples work consistently finds that what helps is not a formula but a responsive, attuned presence, adjusted to the specific people involved (Monson & Fredman, 2012). Use the sentences as scaffolding, then let them become your own.

Two views of the words

Language is where the two panels become almost practical enough to tape to the wall, because for every sentence you might say there is a version of how it may land inside your partner. Holding both views is how you choose the sentence that helps.

What may be happening for your partner. Words may be reaching them at a fraction of their normal strength, so that a long, warm, complex statement arrives as mostly noise. Questions may register as demands for cognitive work they cannot currently do, retrieval and articulation being exactly the capacities that go offline. Reassurance delivered as fact may feel like an argument against their own felt reality, adding shame to fear. Commands, even gentle ones, may echo the powerlessness the old trauma was built around. And silence, if it is calm and unhurried, may communicate safety more effectively than any sentence, because a steady body nearby speaks a language older than words.

What you can safely do from your side. You can make your sentences short, plain, and low in demand, matching your language to what your partner can actually receive. You can trade questions for offers, converting what did I do into we can figure anything out later, and are you okay into I am right here. You can build consent into the words themselves, saying we do not have to talk and there is water if you want it, so that each sentence hands your partner permission rather than a task. You can retire the specific phrases your partner has told you make it worse, in exchange for the ones they have told you help. And you can let silence do the work when silence is what they asked for, choosing one short anchoring sentence and then, harder than it sounds, stopping.

The reason to keep these panels distinct is that the words that feel most loving to say are often the ones that land worst, and only the first panel explains why. Your instinct is written for an ordinary conversation. Your partner, in that moment, is not in an ordinary conversation. The second panel is how you speak to the situation that is actually in front of you.

A question partners ask

Partners sometimes ask what to do when they say the right small sentence and it still does not seem to help, when the calm words land on silence and nothing visibly changes. The answer is that a good sentence in a flashback is not measured by whether it produces an immediate result. Its job is to add no pressure and to signal safety, and it can do that job perfectly while your partner remains, for several more minutes, exactly where they were. You are not looking for a reaction. You are removing a burden. Sometimes the effect of the right sentence is simply that things do not get worse, which is a real and underrated success.

Judge your words by whether they lowered the demand in the room, not by whether they lifted your partner out of the flashback, because lifting them out is not something words can reliably do. The absence of escalation is often the whole win, and it is a win you will only notice if you stop expecting the sentence to be magic.

One Sentence This Week

Your practice this week is deliberately narrow, because narrow practice is how new habits actually form. Choose one sentence, just one, from this chapter, and make it yours. Maybe it is I am here, no rush. Maybe it is we do not have to talk. Say it out loud a few times in private, in the quiet, low, unhurried tone you would want to use, until it feels natural rather than borrowed. Then, the next time a hard moment comes, reach for that one sentence and nothing else. Do not try to deploy the whole chapter. One good sentence, said calmly and then followed by silence, is more than most partners manage, and it is enough. If it helps, ask your partner afterward, in calm, whether that sentence landed well, and let their answer refine it. You are not learning a script. You are learning one true thing to say, and then learning to stop. That second half, the stopping, is the part that will take the most practice, because everything in you will want to keep going, to add, to explain, to fill the quiet with proof of your love. Resist it. One calm sentence followed by steady silence is a more complete act of care than a paragraph, and the discipline of saying less is something you build the same way you build any skill, by doing it badly a few times and then a little better. Your partner does not need your eloquence. They need your steadiness, and steadiness speaks in short sentences. Having found the small language that lowers pressure, you are ready for the moments when words alone are not enough and you have to hold a firm limit while a flashback is still in force. That is where being present stops being sufficient and being clear becomes necessary, and it is where many partners lose their footing. Next, we turn to the harder moments, the ones where you have to hold a limit. Next, we turn to the harder moments, the ones where being present is not enough and you have to hold a limit.

Chapter 5: Boundaries During Activation

There are two mistakes partners make with boundaries, and they look like opposites but come from the same root. The first is having no boundaries at all, absorbing whatever comes, telling yourself that because your partner is in pain you have no right to protect yourself. The second is having only harsh boundaries, drawing lines with anger and threat, punishing your partner for a state they did not choose. Both mistakes come from the same false belief, that compassion and limits cannot occupy the same moment. They can. Learning to hold both at once is the subject of this chapter, and it is one of the most important skills in the book.

The stakes are high because this is where relationships either find their footing or slowly come apart. A partner who never sets a limit becomes exhausted, resentful, and eventually contemptuous, no matter how much they love the person. A partner who sets only cruel limits teaches their traumatized partner that home is another unsafe place. Somewhere between the doormat and the drill sergeant is a third option, and it is available even in the middle of a flashback.

What a boundary actually is

Most of the trouble comes from a basic confusion about what a boundary is. A boundary is a statement about what you will do, not a command about what your partner must do. That distinction sounds academic until you see how much rides on it. I need you to stop yelling is a demand, and demands invite resistance, especially from someone whose sense of control is already threatened. If the yelling continues, I am going to step into the other room is a boundary, because it describes your own action and requires nothing from your partner. You are not controlling them. You are deciding what you will do in response to what they do.

This difference is not a rhetorical trick. It is the whole thing. A demand puts you in a power struggle with a flooded person, which you will lose, because you cannot force a nervous system to obey. A boundary keeps the power where it actually is, with each of you over your own actions. Your partner remains free to keep doing what they are doing, and you remain free to protect yourself from it. Nobody has to win, because you are no longer fighting over the same territory. You have quietly stepped off the battlefield and onto your own ground.

The Kind Fence

The principle here is that a limit and warmth can share a single moment, and stating both at once is not a contradiction. Call it the Kind Fence. A fence marks where your yard ends. It is not an act of aggression against your neighbor. You can build one gently, explain it kindly, and stand behind it without hostility. The same is true of a boundary in a relationship touched by trauma. You can say, in the same breath, that you love your partner and that you will not stay in the room for screaming. Both are true. Saying both is not mixed messaging. It is the accurate message.

The grammar of the Kind Fence usually has two parts, care and limit, and the care comes first. I love you, and I am going to step outside for a few minutes if the shouting keeps up. I want to be here for you, and I cannot do that while I am being called names, so I am going to take a short break and come back. Notice that the limit is about your action, that it names a specific behavior rather than attacking your partner's character, and that it holds the door open for return. That last piece is what separates a boundary from an abandonment. You are not leaving the relationship. You are leaving the shouting, and you are saying you will be back.

Boundaries are not punishment

The most important rule about a boundary is that it is not a weapon. The moment you use a limit to hurt, shame, or control your partner, it stops being a boundary and becomes punishment dressed up as one. Fine, I'm leaving, since you can't control yourself is a punishment. If you're going to act like this, I won't be around is a threat. The words might be similar to a real boundary, but the intent is different, and your partner will feel the difference instantly. A boundary protects you. A punishment tries to harm them into changing. Trauma survivors have often been punished into compliance before, and doing it again, even accidentally, teaches them that you are one more person to fear (Herman, 1992).

This is why tone and timing carry so much of the weight. The same sentence, I am going to step outside, can be a Kind Fence or a slammed door depending on how it is said. Said with calm and care, it protects the relationship. Said with contempt, thrown over your shoulder as you storm out, it wounds. You will not always get this right, because you are a person with your own limits and your own anger, and there will be nights the door does slam. When that happens, it becomes something to repair later, which is a whole chapter of its own. For now, hold the aim: the fence, not the fist.

When accommodation becomes the problem

There is a quieter failure that deserves as much attention as the loud one, because it traps the most devoted partners. It is the slow disappearance of your own limits in the name of helping. You stop seeing friends because leaving feels risky. You stop raising problems because you do not want to upset your partner. You rearrange your entire life around avoiding their distress. This is called accommodation, and research on couples affected by trauma finds that high levels of it are linked to worse outcomes for both people, not better, even though it is done out of love (Fredman et al., 2014).

Accommodation feels like generosity, but past a certain point it becomes a kind of erasure, and it does not even work. Organizing everything around preventing flashbacks does not prevent them, and it quietly teaches both of you that your partner is too fragile to encounter an ordinary life. It also builds a hidden reservoir of resentment that eventually poisons the care it was meant to express. The couple adaptation to trauma model describes how a traumatic stress can reorganize a whole relationship system, sometimes in ways that keep both partners stuck (Nelson Goff & Smith, 2005). The Kind Fence is part of how you stay a full person inside a relationship that could otherwise swallow you.

Maevren keeps his evening

Maevren, fifty-two, had gradually given up his Thursday chess night, the one reliable pleasure in his week, because his partner Virel, fifty, sometimes had hard evenings and he felt he should be home in case. He did not decide this all at once. It happened one cancellation at a time, each one reasonable on its own, until the night was simply gone and he was quietly furious about a loss he had chosen. The resentment leaked into everything, and Virel could feel it without knowing its source, which made her own hard evenings worse.

What changed was not dramatic. Maevren told Virel, in calm, that he was going back to chess night, that he loved her, and that he would have his phone if she truly needed him but that he was no longer going to cancel by default. He braced for her to fall apart. She did not. She was relieved, because his hovering had felt to her like being treated as an invalid. Their first Thursday apart was awkward and both of them checked their phones too much, and it was still better than the arrangement that had been hollowing him out. The fence gave him back a piece of himself, and it gave her back a partner rather than a nurse.

The limit that is never negotiable

Everything in this chapter assumes a certain range of difficulty, hard flashbacks with raised voices and painful words, the ordinary storms of a trauma-affected relationship. There is a limit that sits outside that range and is never up for negotiation, and I will name it here and return to it fully at the end of the book. A trauma history explains behavior. It never obligates you to accept behavior that endangers you. If a flashback involves physical aggression, threats to your safety, or anything that makes you genuinely afraid for your body, the boundary is not a chess night. It is your safety, and it comes first, always, without guilt. Most people with post-traumatic stress are never violent, and holding that line is not a betrayal of the people who are not (Elbogen & Johnson, 2009; Taft et al., 2011). We will treat this carefully in Chapter 10. For now, simply hold it as the floor beneath every other boundary: care has limits, and safety is where they stop being optional.

You are not their regulator

Underneath the fear of setting boundaries is usually a belief worth dragging into the light, because it runs so many partners into the ground. The belief is that it is your job to keep your partner regulated, that if they have a flashback you have failed, that their emotional state is your responsibility to manage. It is not. You can support, offer, steady, and stay. You cannot regulate another adult's nervous system for them, and trying to becomes a trap that exhausts you and infantilizes them. Their recovery is their own, supported by their own work and, ideally, their own clinician, and there is real reason for hope, because the symptoms of complex trauma do respond to appropriate treatment (Karatzias et al., 2019). Your boundaries are not obstacles to their healing. Boundaries from a calm, caring partner are part of the safe, real relationship that supports healing in the first place (Monson & Fredman, 2012).

Two views of a boundary

Boundaries are where partners most fear they are being cruel, so the two panels are especially worth holding here, because a kind fence lands very differently inside your partner than the punishment it can be mistaken for.

What may be happening for your partner. A limit stated with warmth may register as safety rather than rejection, because it makes the relationship predictable, and predictability is steadying for a nervous system braced for threat. A limit stated with contempt, by contrast, may land as one more person becoming unsafe, echoing the punishment-into-compliance that many survivors have lived through before. Your accommodation, the quiet dissolving of your own limits, may feel to them not like generosity but like being treated as fragile, an invalid to be managed rather than a partner to be lived with. And a boundary that names a behavior rather than attacking their character may be something they can actually take in, because it does not require them to defend who they are.

What you can safely do from your side. You can state a boundary as a description of your own action, I am going to step outside for a few minutes, rather than a command about theirs. You can lead with care and follow with the limit, in the same breath, so that both truths are present. You can name the specific behavior rather than the person, holding the line against the shouting without a verdict on their worth. You can hold the door open for return, so that a boundary never becomes an abandonment. And you can keep the non-negotiable floor firmly in view, the line at your own physical safety, which no amount of trauma or love ever moves.

The first panel is what frees you to set boundaries at all, because it shows that a kind fence is not a withdrawal of love but a form of it. The second panel is how you build the fence without turning it into a weapon. Kept together, they let you be both caring and clear, which is the entire skill of this chapter.

This week

Your practice this week is to identify one boundary you have quietly let dissolve, and to notice it without yet acting. Look for the thing you used to do, or the topic you used to raise, or the small piece of your life you have given up to keep the peace. You do not have to reclaim it this week. You just have to see it clearly and name it to yourself: this is a fence I stopped maintaining. Seeing the accommodation is the necessary first step, because you cannot rebuild a fence you have convinced yourself was never there. If you feel ready, plan one sentence you might use to begin restoring it, care first, limit second, in language you could say with warmth.

A question partners ask

A frequent question is what to do when a boundary, however kindly stated, seems to escalate the flashback rather than calm it. Sometimes naming a limit does raise the temperature briefly, because a flooded person may experience even a gentle boundary as one more pressure. This does not mean the boundary was wrong. It means you may need to state it once, calmly, and then stop defending or repeating it, letting your action speak instead of your words. If you said you would step into the other room when the shouting continued, then step into the other room, quietly, without a lecture attached. The boundary was never a request for your partner's agreement. It was a description of what you would do, and doing it, calmly and without punishment, is the boundary. Repeating and arguing for a limit turns it back into a demand, which is the very thing you were trying to avoid. State it kindly, once, and then act on it. The action is the fence, not the announcement.

Fence and Warmth

It is worth ending on the reframe that makes all of this possible, because partners so often experience boundaries and love as a tradeoff, as though every limit is a small withdrawal of care. It is the reverse. A relationship with no fences is not more loving. It is more chaotic, more resentful, and less safe for both people. The fence is what makes the yard a place you can actually live. When you hold a kind limit, you are not loving your partner less. You are building the kind of steady, honest relationship in which their trauma has room to heal and your own self has room to survive. Warmth without a fence burns out. A fence without warmth wounds. The two together, held in the same moment, are what this work is made of. Neither one is optional. A partner who offers only warmth becomes exhausted and eventually resentful, and a partner who offers only fences becomes cold and frightening, and the person you love needs you to be neither of those. The skill is the both-at-once, the care and the limit in a single breath, and it is a skill precisely because it does not come naturally under stress. You will get it wrong on the hard nights and closer to right on the calmer ones, and both are part of learning it. Sometimes, though, the kindest fence of all is distance, and knowing when to take space is the subject of the next chapter.

Chapter 6: When Space Is the Better Answer

When does stepping away help, and when does it wound? That single question keeps more partners paralyzed than almost any other, because the same action, walking out of the room, can be the most caring thing you do or the most damaging, and from the outside the two look identical. A partner who leaves to protect a fragile moment and a partner who leaves to abandon one both walk through the same door. The difference is everything, and it is not in the leaving. It is in what surrounds the leaving.

This chapter is about doing distance well. Space is a real tool, sometimes the best one, and partners who never use it burn out or make hard moments worse by crowding them. But space done badly, taken suddenly, without agreement, with no plan to return, can confirm the deepest fear a traumatized person carries, which is that closeness is unreliable and people leave. So we have to separate the healthy pause from the wound that looks like it, and the separation comes down to one idea.

The Agreed Distance

Space chosen together, in advance, is care. Space taken alone, in the heat, without warning, often reads as abandonment even when it is not. The principle is the Agreed Distance: the time to decide how you will take space is not during a flashback but long before one, in calm, together. A pause you both designed and consented to is a shared plan you are executing. A pause you improvise mid-crisis is a unilateral exit your partner did not agree to and may experience as being left. The action can be the same. The meaning is opposite, and the meaning is set by whether it was agreed.

This is why so much of the work happens outside the hard moments. In the calm, you and your partner can build a simple understanding: when things get to a certain point, one of us may need to step away, here is what that will look like, and here is how we will come back. Because you built it together, when the moment comes and you say I am going to take the break we talked about, you are not leaving. You are keeping an agreement. Your partner, even flooded, has a frame for what is happening, and the frame is we planned for this, not they are gone.

What a good time-out contains

An agreed pause has a few parts, and each one matters. It has a signal, a short phrase either of you can use that means I need a break now, chosen so it does not sound like an insult. It has a duration, a rough sense of how long, because open-ended disappearance is frightening and a stated time is reassuring. It has a location, so no one is wondering where the other went. And it has a re-contact plan, an agreement about who will check back in and when, so the person left behind is not abandoned to the silence. Trauma so often involves the terror of not knowing what is coming next, and every one of these parts reduces that terror by making the pause predictable (Herman, 1992).

The re-contact plan is the piece partners most often forget, and it is the piece that turns a pause into care rather than a cliffhanger. Twenty minutes of space with I will come check on you in twenty minutes attached feels completely different from twenty minutes of space with nothing attached. In the first, your partner is waiting for a known return. In the second, they are alone with the question of whether you are ever coming back, which for someone with an abandonment wound is its own flashback waiting to happen. The promise of return is what makes the leaving safe.

What not to do during a pause

There are ways to take space that quietly sabotage it, and they are worth naming because they are common. Do not use the pause to stew, building your case, sharpening your grievances, so that you return angrier than you left. The pause is for settling, not for prosecuting. Do not disappear further than agreed, driving off when you said you would be in the next room, because moving the goalposts mid-pause breaks the very predictability that made it safe. Do not use the silence to punish, letting the break stretch past its agreed length to make a point. And do not come back before you are actually calm, because returning while still flooded restarts the whole thing.

Use the space to do the work of the earlier chapters on yourself. Slow your body. Let your own alarm come down. A pause is often as much for the supporting partner's nervous system as for the partner with trauma, because you cannot offer steadiness from a body that is still braced (van der Kolk, 2014). When you come back regulated rather than merely cooled off, you bring the calm the moment needs. The quality of your return depends almost entirely on what you did during the break, and the best thing you can do during a break is get yourself genuinely settled.

Sevrin's twenty minutes

Sevrin, twenty-seven, and their partner had worked out an agreed pause after too many nights that ended with someone storming off. Their plan was plain: either could say I need our twenty, one of them would go to the bedroom, the other would stay in the living room, and whoever called the break would come back after twenty minutes to check in. The first time they used it for real, Sevrin was shaking and certain it would feel like rejection to say the phrase out loud. They said it anyway. Their partner nodded, which was all the nervous system could manage, and the two of them separated.

Those twenty minutes were not comfortable. Sevrin sat on the bed doubting the whole arrangement, sure they had just made everything worse. But when they returned, on time, their partner was calmer, and the fact that Sevrin had come back exactly when they said they would was itself a kind of proof, a small piece of evidence that this pause was not the beginning of a disappearance. Over months, that repeated proof did something no single conversation could. It slowly taught both of them that stepping away and coming back was survivable, even ordinary. The agreement worked because they had built it in calm and honored it in the storm.

When it goes wrong

It does not always go like Sevrin's. Cyrel, forty-one, whom you have been following, had a night that went badly, and it is worth telling because his failure is more instructive than anyone's success. He and Éloane, thirty-nine, had talked loosely about taking space but had never actually built the agreement, no signal, no duration, no re-contact plan. So when a flashback turned into a painful argument and Cyrel felt his own control slipping, he did what felt like the responsible thing. He grabbed his keys and left. He drove around for an hour to calm down. In his mind, he was protecting them both from something worse.

Éloane experienced it as the floor giving way. She did not know where he had gone, when or whether he would return, or what his leaving meant. The silence filled with the oldest story her trauma told, that people leave and closeness cannot be trusted, and by the time Cyrel came home, calm and proud of having avoided a blowup, she was far past where the original flashback had left her. His unplanned exit had confirmed her deepest fear. The space itself had not been the problem. The absence of agreement had turned a reasonable need into a wound.

They did not recover from that night quickly, and I want to be honest that some damage takes real time to mend. What they did do, a week later, once things had settled, was finally build the agreement they had skipped, with all its parts, including the re-contact promise Cyrel's instinct had entirely missed. The next time he needed space, months on, he took it differently, and it went better, though not perfectly, because Éloane still felt an echo of the earlier night. The repair was partial. That is what real repair usually is, and it is the subject of a later chapter. The lesson here is narrower and it is this: the space Cyrel took was not wrong, but taking it without an agreement made it land as the thing he was trying to prevent.

Space is not the enemy of closeness

It would be easy to take the wrong lesson from Cyrel's night and conclude that taking space is dangerous. That is not the lesson. Partners who refuse to ever step away, who force themselves to stay present through every storm no matter their own state, do not build closer relationships. They build more explosive ones, because two flooded people in the same small room have nowhere to go but into each other. The window of tolerance is real for you as well as your partner, and honoring your own limits by stepping away is often what prevents the worst outcomes (Siegel, 1999). Space, done with agreement, is not the opposite of connection. It is one of the things that protects it.

The deeper point is that closeness and distance are not enemies. A relationship needs both, and a trauma-affected relationship needs the ability to move between them on purpose, without either one meaning catastrophe. The Agreed Distance is how you make distance safe, so that taking it does not cost you closeness and staying close does not cost you your sanity. When space is available and agreed, you both stop fearing it, and a great deal of the pressure drains out of your hard moments simply because there is a known exit that is not an ending.

Two views of taking space

Space is the tool most likely to be experienced as its opposite, so the two panels earn their keep here more than anywhere. The same walk out of the room can be care or wound depending on which inner experience it meets.

What may be happening for your partner. An unplanned exit may confirm the oldest story their trauma tells, that closeness is unreliable and people leave, so that the space itself becomes a fresh injury on top of the original one. Not knowing where you have gone, or for how long, or whether you are coming back, may fill the silence with a fear as large as the flashback that started it. An agreed pause, by contrast, may be experienced as a shared plan being executed rather than an abandonment, because they helped design it and know how it ends. And the simple fact of you returning exactly when you said you would may become, over time, a piece of evidence that stepping away and coming back is survivable, which is its own quiet healing.

What you can safely do from your side. You can build the pause agreement in calm, with a signal, a duration, a location, and above all a re-contact plan, so that the space you take later is a promise rather than a disappearance. You can name the pause as the one you both agreed on, giving your partner a frame even when they are flooded. You can use the break to settle your own body rather than to build your case, so that you return regulated rather than merely cooled off. You can honor the agreed length exactly, neither cutting it short nor stretching it to punish. And you can keep the promise of return, because the return is what makes the leaving safe.

The first panel is why space done badly does so much damage, and the second is how you make space that connects rather than severs. Cyrel learned the first panel the hard way, by living it. You get to learn it here, which is cheaper.

This week

Your practice this week is to draft a pause agreement with your partner, in calm, with all four parts. Pick the signal phrase together, something neutral that will not sting when said in a hard moment. Agree on a rough duration. Decide where each of you will go. And most of all, write in the re-contact plan, who checks back and when, because that is the part that turns leaving into a promise of return. Do not test it during a crisis this week. Just build it, out loud, together, so that it exists before you need it. An agreement made in calm is a gift you are handing your future selves for a night you cannot yet see.

A question partners ask

Partners often ask how to take space when their partner follows them, unable to tolerate the separation, so that the pause never actually happens. This is real, and it is why the re-contact plan and the stated duration matter so much, because they give the following partner something to hold onto other than pursuit. If your partner cannot yet bear even a short, agreed pause, that is important information, not a failure of the method, and it usually points to an abandonment fear that deserves gentleness rather than force. You can shorten the pause, keep it within sight rather than behind a closed door, or check in more frequently, adjusting the agreement to what your partner can currently tolerate. Over time, as the repeated experience of you leaving briefly and returning reliably accumulates, most couples find that longer and more separate pauses become possible. You are not failing if the first version of your pause is very small. You are building tolerance for separation one honored return at a time.

The Door You Left Open

Come back to the image that opened this chapter, the door that both the caring partner and the abandoning partner walk through. What separates them, you now know, is not the door. It is whether the door was left open, whether there was an agreement to return, whether the person left behind knew the leaving had an end. An agreed pause is a door left open. You step through it, and both of you know you are coming back, because you said so, in calm, before the storm ever arrived. That open door is what makes space an act of care. Without it, distance is just distance, and distance without a promise of return is the exact shape of the fear your partner is already carrying. With it, distance becomes something the two of you can use on purpose, a tool rather than a threat, available whenever a hard moment needs more room than the same four walls can give. The agreement is small to build and large in what it prevents, and it is one of the few things in this book you can put in place entirely in advance, before you ever need it. And when you walk back through it, calmer, keeping the promise you made, you arrive at the next piece of the work, which is how two people actually come back together after the hard moment has passed.

Chapter 7: Coming Back Into the Relationship

Partners of people with post-traumatic stress report more relationship distress and more of their own distress than partners of people without it, a finding that holds across many studies (Lambert et al., 2012). When you read a sentence like that, it is easy to picture the distress living in the loud moments, the flashbacks and the fights. But a great deal of it actually lives in the quiet afterward, in the awkward, unrepaired hours that follow a hard night. The flashback ends, the storm passes, and then the couple is left with a strange, careful distance that no one knows how to cross. That crossing is what this chapter is about. Post-traumatic stress is, in fact, among the conditions most strongly associated with relationship difficulty at a population level (Kessler, 2000), and much of that difficulty is decided in exactly these quiet, unrepaired hours.

Most couples handle the aftermath badly, not through any failure of love but through not knowing there is a skill to it. The two common mistakes are opposite and both painful. One is pretending nothing happened, sliding back into normal life with a false brightness while the hard moment sits unaddressed between you like furniture no one mentions. The other is rushing straight into processing, wanting to talk it all through immediately, demanding understanding and resolution while both nervous systems are still raw. The first leaves the wound uncleaned. The second reopens it. Between them is a better way.

Why coming back is its own event

It helps to understand that reconnection after a flashback is not automatic and should not be. When a hard moment ends, your partner is not instantly back to baseline, and neither are you. The body takes time to come down from a threat state, and pushing for closeness before that settling is complete is like trying to shake hands with someone who is still catching their breath (Ogden et al., 2006). The end of the flashback is not the end of the episode. There is a recovery period afterward, often longer than the flashback itself, and reconnection has to respect it.

This is why coming back deserves to be treated as its own distinct event, with its own timing and its own gentleness, rather than as an afterthought. In the moment, you were focused on safety and steadiness. Now the task is different. It is to rebuild the ordinary closeness that the hard moment interrupted, and to do it in a way that does not demand more from either of you than you have yet recovered. Rushing this is how couples end up relitigating the flashback and starting a second one. Skipping it entirely is how couples slowly become roommates who share a history of unspoken bad nights.

The Re-Entry Ramp

The principle is that reconnection needs a threshold, not a leap. Call it the Re-Entry Ramp. You do not go from the far edge of a flashback straight back to full emotional intimacy in one jump. You come up a ramp, in small steps, starting with the lowest-demand contact and moving toward closeness only as both of you can tolerate it. The first step back is not a conversation. It is presence. Simply being in the same space again, doing something ordinary, without any pressure to talk about what happened, is the bottom of the ramp, and it is often enough for a while.

The ramp has a rough order. First, shared space with no demand, being in the same room, maybe doing separate things. Then, small ordinary exchanges, a comment about dinner, a question about the dog, the low-stakes talk of a normal evening. Then, if both of you seem ready, a small gesture of warmth, a touch on the shoulder offered and not forced, a softening of tone. Only later, sometimes not until the next day, does the ramp reach the top, where you might actually talk about what happened. Trying to start at the top is the error. You start at the bottom, and you let your partner's responses tell you how fast to climb.

Reading the readiness

The ramp only works if you read your partner rather than run a timetable, because recovery does not keep a schedule. Some nights the climb is quick and you are back to easy closeness within the hour. Some nights your partner needs the whole evening at the bottom of the ramp, present but not pushed, and any attempt to move faster stalls things out. You learn to read the small signs of readiness, the same kind of signals you mapped in Chapter 2 but running in reverse: the voice softening, the body turning back toward you, the first joke, the first genuine question about your day. These are invitations up the ramp, and when they come, you can take the next small step.

What you do not do is announce the ramp or narrate it. You do not say I think you're ready for the next level of reconnection now. You simply offer the next small thing and watch whether it is received. If a light comment lands and gets a real response, the ramp is open. If it falls flat, you drop back down a step and wait. This responsiveness, offering and reading, offering and reading, is the actual skill, and it matters far more than any fixed sequence. The Gottman research on lasting relationships found that couples who repair well are those who make and receive small bids for connection, over and over, rather than one grand reconciliation (Gottman & Silver, 1999). The ramp is a series of small bids.

Aeris and the un-rushed evening

Aeris, thirty-eight, used to treat the end of a flashback as a starting gun. The instant her partner seemed a little better, she wanted to talk it through, to understand, to fix, to get back to okay. Her urgency, she eventually realized, was mostly about her own discomfort with the lingering distance, and it consistently backfired, launching second arguments out of the ashes of the first. What changed her was an experiment in doing almost nothing. One evening, after a hard episode, she made herself simply exist in the same room, folding laundry, saying nothing about what had happened, offering only the most ordinary presence.

It was excruciating for her, and it worked better than anything she had tried. After a while her partner drifted over and started helping with the laundry, and they folded in silence for a few minutes, and that shared, wordless task was the whole reconciliation. There was no big talk that night, and Aeris had to sit with the discomfort of an unresolved evening. But the closeness came back, quietly, up the ramp, at her partner's pace instead of hers. The talk, when it eventually happened, came two days later and went well, in part because it was not forced into the raw hours right after the storm.

When there does need to be a talk

Sometimes the flashback involved words or actions that genuinely need addressing, and the ramp does eventually reach a real conversation. When it does, timing is the whole thing. The conversation belongs at the top of the ramp, when both of you are settled, rested, and back inside your windows, which often means the next day, not the same night. Trying to process while still raw is the single most common way couples turn one hard moment into two (Monson & Fredman, 2012). Waiting is not avoidance. Waiting is choosing the moment when the conversation can actually be useful instead of the moment when it can only do damage.

That later conversation is where repair happens, and repair is involved enough to deserve its own chapter, which is where we go next. For now, the point is only that the talk has a proper place, and its proper place is up the ramp and often across a night's sleep, not in the smoking aftermath of the episode. If your partner is not ready to talk when you are, the readiness of the more raw person sets the pace. You can hold your need for the conversation without imposing it, and holding it a little longer almost always makes the eventual talk go better.

Solenne and Auren find a rhythm

Solenne and Auren, whom you have followed since the first chapter, had by this point built something like a rhythm for coming back, and it is worth seeing because it was ordinary rather than impressive. After a hard moment, they had a small, wordless ritual: Solenne would put the kettle on. It meant nothing and everything. It was the bottom of the ramp, a way of being in the same space doing something normal, and it asked nothing of Auren. Sometimes he stayed at the far edge for a long while and the tea went cold. Sometimes he came and sat with her within minutes. The kettle did not control which, and that was the point. It was an offer, not a demand.

Their rhythm was not a triumph and I do not want to present it as one. There were still nights the reconnection failed, when Auren stayed shut down until sleep and they woke up to an unrepaired distance that took days to close. What they had was not a solution but a practice, a way of reaching for each other after the storm that worked often enough to keep the relationship warm. That is what a good re-entry ramp gives you. Not a guarantee that every hard night ends in closeness, but a reliable, low-pressure way to try, one that does not add a second injury to the first.

Two views of coming back

Reconnection has its own version of the two panels, and holding them is how you avoid the twin errors of pretending nothing happened and rushing to process everything at once.

What may be happening for your partner. Their body may still be coming down from the threat state well after the flashback itself has passed, so that they are not yet ready for the closeness you are ready for. They may feel exposed or ashamed about what happened, afraid they have damaged something, which can make them wary of contact even as they want it. A push to talk it all through immediately may feel like being asked to climb back into the fire before they have caught their breath. Low-demand presence, being in the same room doing something ordinary, may be exactly what they can tolerate and welcome. And they may need the actual conversation to wait until the next day, not as avoidance but as the only timing at which it can go well.

What you can safely do from your side. You can start at the bottom of the ramp with shared space and no demand, letting your presence be the first offer. You can make small, ordinary bids for connection and read whether they are received, moving up only as your partner's responses invite it. You can offer warmth as a gesture rather than a requirement, a touch that can be accepted or declined. You can resist the urge to process in the raw hours, holding your own need for the conversation until the top of the ramp, often the next day. And you can let the readiness of the more raw person set the pace, which is a form of respect, not a loss.

The first panel keeps you patient by explaining why your partner is not moving at your speed. The second gives you something to actually do with that patience, so that waiting becomes an active, skillful offer rather than a helpless stall. Together they turn the lonely aftermath into a shared, gradual return.

This week

Your practice this week is to design your own bottom-of-the-ramp gesture, the small, ordinary, no-demand thing you can offer after a hard moment. It should ask nothing of your partner and carry no pressure to talk. Solenne had her kettle. Aeris had her laundry. Yours might be putting on quiet music, starting to cook, sitting down with a book in the same room. Choose it now, in calm, so that when the moment comes you are not improvising. Then, if a hard moment happens this week, resist every urge to talk it through immediately, and instead offer only your small gesture and see what your partner does with it. You are practicing starting at the bottom of the ramp instead of leaping for the top.

A question partners ask

Partners sometimes ask what to do when they are ready to reconnect but their partner stays shut down for hours or even into the next day, leaving them alone with the unresolved evening. The answer is that the ramp has no fixed timetable, and the more raw person sets the pace, which sometimes means the pace is very slow. Your job in that stretch is to keep the bottom of the ramp available, an ordinary, no-demand presence, without escalating your bids or letting your own hurt harden into withdrawal. It is genuinely lonely to hold the memory of the hard moment while your partner recovers, and you are allowed to tend your own feelings during it, ideally with support of your own. What you are not required to do is force the reconnection or punish its slowness. The closeness usually returns, even when it takes until morning, and the nights it does not simply become episodes that need repair, which is a skill and not a catastrophe. Patience here is not passivity. It is the offer.

When You Both Come Back

I want to end this chapter by speaking to you directly, because the aftermath of a flashback is a lonely place for the supporting partner and it rarely gets acknowledged. You are the one holding the memory of the hard moment while your partner is still recovering from it, and that can leave you carrying the whole weight of the evening alone, waiting, unsure whether the closeness will return. It usually does, if you let the ramp do its work and do not force the climb. The coming back is real, even when it is slow, even when it is wordless, even when it takes until morning. And on the nights it does not come back the way you hoped, that is not the end of anything. It is simply an episode that needs repair, and repair is a skill you can learn. No single hard night, left briefly unmended, is a verdict on your relationship. Couples survive unresolved evenings all the time, and what carries them is not a spotless record but the reliable knowledge that hard moments can be mended when both people are ready. That knowledge is built one repair at a time. The couples who last are not the ones who never have a bad night that fails to mend by morning. They are the ones who trust, from long experience, that mending is possible even when it is delayed, and who return to the work of repair rather than filing each unresolved night away as evidence against the relationship. Building that trust is exactly where we turn next.

Chapter 8: Repair Without a Courtroom

I should confess something, because it is relevant and because pretending otherwise would be dishonest. For years, in my own life, I treated the conversation after a fight as a trial. I came to it with evidence. I wanted a verdict. I wanted it established, on the record, who had done what and who was therefore responsible, as though love were a matter to be settled by proof. It did not work, not once, and it took me an embarrassingly long time to understand why. A relationship is not a courtroom, and the moment you turn a repair into a trial, both of you have already lost, because the only possible outcomes are a guilty party and an acquittal, and neither one is closeness.

This chapter is about repairing after a hard moment in a way that does not require anyone to win. It is the most involved skill in the book, and it is the one that determines, more than any other, whether your relationship grows sturdier through hard moments or slowly erodes under them. Couples who repair well are not couples who have fewer conflicts. They are couples who have learned to reconnect afterward without turning the reconnection into a rematch (Gottman & Silver, 1999). The good news is that repair is a skill, not a talent, and its central move can be stated simply.

Why the same fight repeats

Start with the pattern that probably brought you to this chapter, the fight you keep having, the one that circles back no matter how many times you think you have settled it. Circular fights almost always come from a confusion of categories. The two of you are trying to resolve several different questions at once, all tangled together, and because you never separate them, you can never settle any of them. Who was hurt, who meant what, who is responsible for what, what part trauma played, and what happens now are five distinct questions, and jammed into one argument they become an unsolvable knot.

Trauma makes this knot tighter, because a flashback introduces a genuinely complicating fact: some of what happened was driven by an alarm no one chose. That fact can be misused in both directions. It can become an excuse that erases all responsibility, it was just my trauma, so nothing I did counts. Or it can be ignored entirely, as though the flashback were a fully deliberate choice. Neither is true, and the circular fight often is really a struggle over which of those distortions gets to stand. Untangling the knot means pulling the questions apart and answering them separately, and the first pair to separate is the one that causes the most damage.

The Two Truths of Repair

Here is the principle at the center of this chapter, and it is worth reading slowly. Impact and intent are both real, and neither one cancels the other. Call it the Two Truths of Repair. When your partner's flashback led to words that hurt you, two things are true at the same time. The hurt you feel is real and valid, and your partner very likely did not intend it. Most couples treat these as opponents, as though acknowledging the lack of intent means dismissing the hurt, or acknowledging the hurt means assigning malicious intent. They are not opponents. They are simply two facts, and repair begins the moment you can hold both without making them fight.

This is the move that dissolves the courtroom. In a trial, intent and impact are on trial together, and one must defeat the other. In a repair, they sit side by side. You can say to your partner, that really hurt me, and I know you were not trying to hurt me, in the same breath, and mean both halves completely. Your partner can say, I did not mean to hurt you, and I can see that I did, and I am sorry, without the apology requiring them to have been a villain. The hurt gets acknowledged. The intent gets acknowledged. Nobody has to be the guilty party, because you have stopped running a trial.

Pulling the five questions apart

Once you can hold the two truths, the rest of the knot comes loose more easily, and it helps to name the five questions and take them in order. First, impact: what actually hurt, said plainly and owned as your experience, not as an accusation. Second, intent: an honest look at what your partner was actually trying to do, which in a flashback was usually to survive a feeling, not to wound you. Third, responsibility: not for the flashback, which no one chooses, but for the specific words or actions and for the repair, which everyone can own regardless of cause. Fourth, trauma history: the context that explains without excusing, the old alarm that helps you both understand why the moment went the way it did. Fifth, repair: what each of you can do now and next time.

The reason to keep these separate is that they get different answers, and jamming them together forces a single wrong answer onto all five. Your partner is not responsible for having a flashback and is responsible for the repair. The trauma history explains the harshness and does not excuse you having to absorb it. The impact is real and the intent was not malicious. Each of these is true on its own line, and it is only when you smear them into one line that they seem to contradict. Clinicians who work with trauma-affected couples spend a great deal of time helping partners make exactly these distinctions, because the distinctions are what let a couple stop relitigating and start healing (Monson & Fredman, 2012).

Responsibility is not the same as blame

The word that trips couples most is responsibility, because it gets confused with blame, and they are not the same. Blame looks backward and asks whose fault it was. Responsibility looks forward and asks who will do what now. Your partner can take responsibility for the repair, for the apology, for trying something different next time, without any of that meaning the flashback was their fault. You can take responsibility for your part, for the pursuing or the correcting or the words you also said in the heat, without that meaning the whole thing was on you.

Responsibility divided this way is not a distribution of guilt. It is a distribution of the work of moving forward.

This reframe matters especially because trauma survivors often carry a heavy, distorted sense of blame already, a tendency to feel that everything is their fault, which is part of the negative self-concept that can accompany complex trauma (Cloitre et al., 2018). If your repairs slide into blame, you feed that distortion, and a partner drowning in self-blame cannot do the forward work of repair. Keeping responsibility separate from blame protects your partner from the shame spiral and keeps them able to participate. You are not letting anyone off the hook. You are pointing everyone at the hook that actually matters, which is what happens next.

Alaris and Noélin repair a hard night

Alaris, forty-four, and Noélin, forty-two, had a specific bad night to repair. During a flashback, Noélin had said something cutting about Alaris's family, something that landed in a tender place, and Alaris had spent the following day cold and withdrawn, quietly building the case for the prosecution. When they finally sat down, at the top of the ramp, a full day later, Alaris's first instinct was to present the evidence. What changed the conversation was that he had been practicing the two truths, and he led with both halves instead of one.

He told Noélin that what she said about his family had genuinely hurt, and that he also knew she had been in a flashback and had not been aiming at him. Noélin, braced for a trial, was disarmed by not being on trial. She was able to say that she was sorry, that she could see the hurt, and that she did not actually believe the thing she had said. Then they did the harder work of separating the questions, and Alaris admitted his day of icy withdrawal had been its own kind of harm, his responsibility to own. It was not a perfect conversation. Alaris still felt a residue of the hurt for a while afterward, because real feelings do not resolve on a schedule. But they repaired, genuinely, and the fight did not become one of the circular ones, because they had refused to hold court.

When repair is one-sided

There is a hard reality to name, because pretending repair is always mutual would set you up for disappointment. Sometimes your partner cannot yet participate in repair the way this chapter describes. The shame is too big, the skills are not there yet, the trauma is too active. On those occasions, you may find yourself doing more of the repair work than feels fair, extending understanding you are not receiving in equal measure. This is real, and it is worth being honest with yourself about how sustainable it is, which is the subject of the next chapter.

What you can do, even when repair is lopsided, is refuse to make it worse. You can decline the courtroom even if your partner cannot yet join you outside it. You can hold the two truths on your own side, acknowledging both your hurt and their likely lack of intent, without waiting for them to acknowledge either. This is not the same as accepting everything. It is choosing, for now, to keep the door to repair open even when your partner cannot walk through it yet. There are limits to how long you can sustain this on your own, and finding those limits is not a failure of love, but within them, refusing to hold court is something you can do regardless of what your partner does.

Repair is a practice, not an event

One repair does not fix a relationship, and expecting it to will exhaust you. Repair is a practice you return to, again and again, getting slightly better at holding the two truths, slightly quicker to separate the questions, slightly less prone to prosecute. The couples who do well are not the ones who repair perfectly. They are the ones who keep repairing, who treat each hard moment as another chance to practice rather than another entry in the case file (Gottman & Silver, 1999). What accumulates over time is not a spotless record but a growing trust that hard moments can be survived and mended, and that trust is worth more than any single flawless conversation.

Two views of the repair

Even repair, which happens when both of you are calmer, benefits from the two panels, because the way a repair conversation lands inside your partner is not the same as the way it feels to conduct.

What may be happening for your partner. They may carry a heavy, distorted sense that everything is their fault, part of the negative self-concept that often accompanies complex trauma, so that any hint of blame can tip them into a shame spiral where repair becomes impossible. They may fear that acknowledging the impact of their words means being convicted as a villain, which can make them defensive when what they actually want is to make things right. They may not yet have the skills or the steadiness to participate in repair as fully as you can, so that the work is temporarily lopsided. And they may be genuinely relieved to be met with both truths at once, to hear that the hurt was real and that their lack of intent is also seen, because that combination is the one thing that lets them stay in the conversation.

What you can safely do from your side. You can lead with both truths, naming the impact and acknowledging the intent in the same breath, so that your partner is met rather than tried. You can separate the five questions, keeping responsibility distinct from blame and trauma-history distinct from excuse, so the knot comes loose. You can own your own part, the pursuing or the withdrawing or the words you also said, without making the whole thing yours. You can hold the two truths on your own side even when your partner cannot yet join you outside the courtroom. And you can treat repair as a practice you return to rather than a verdict you deliver once, getting slightly better each time.

The first panel is why gentleness in repair is not softness but strategy, because a partner in a shame spiral cannot repair at all. The second is how you keep the conversation out of the courtroom regardless of whether your partner is ready to leave it too.

This week

Your practice this week is to say the two truths out loud, in a real repair, even a small one. You do not need a dramatic flashback to practice on.

The next time any hard moment leaves a mark, wait for the top of the ramp, then open with both halves: name the impact honestly, and acknowledge the likely intent, in the same breath. That really landed hard for me, and I know you were not trying to do that. Then stop, and let your partner respond to being met instead of tried. You are practicing the single move that turns a courtroom back into a relationship, and it starts with refusing to make either truth defeat the other.

A question partners ask

A hard question partners raise is what to do when they hold both truths, lead with impact and intent, do everything this chapter asks, and their partner still cannot repair, still deflects or shuts down or turns it back on them. The honest answer is that you cannot repair alone, and one person holding the two truths does not guarantee the other can meet them. What you can do is decline the courtroom on your side, refuse to prosecute even when repair is not returned, and be clear-eyed about how sustainable a lopsided pattern is over time. A single unreturned repair is ordinary. A steady, long-term pattern in which repair is always your job and never your partner's is worth taking seriously, both for your own wellbeing and as information about the relationship. Bringing that pattern to your own therapist or a couples clinician is not disloyal. It is what people do when a skill they are practicing keeps meeting a wall. You can keep the door to repair open without agreeing to be the only one who ever walks through it.

Two Things at Once

The whole of this chapter reduces to a capacity that sounds simple and is not: the ability to hold two things at once. Your hurt and their innocence of intent. Their responsibility and their blamelessness for the flashback. The explanation and the accountability. Trauma pushes couples toward single answers, toward someone being simply right and someone being simply wrong, because single answers feel safer when everything is raw. Repair asks for the harder, truer thing, which is to let two facts be true together and neither one win. When you can do that, the courtroom empties, and what is left is two people who had a hard night and are finding their way back to each other. Doing that, again and again, is demanding work, and it raises a question this book has circled from the start, which is who is taking care of the person doing all this caring. That is where we go now.

Chapter 9: Protecting the Supporting Partner

The tiredness that does not lift after sleep. The resentment you are ashamed of. The friends you have not called in months. The sense that you have become a manager of someone else's moods and lost track of your own. The startle you feel now at raised voices, even on television. The way you scan a room, any room, for signs of trouble. The quiet grief for the relationship you thought you were going to have. If you recognize even a few of these, this chapter is the most important one in the book for you, because it is the one that is actually about you, and it has been coming since the first page.

For eight chapters you have been learning to take care of your partner. Now we turn the attention around, and not as an afterthought or a reward for good behavior. Taking care of yourself is not the nice extra at the end. It is a load-bearing part of the whole structure, because a depleted supporter cannot sustain support, and a supporter who disappears into the role does no one any good, least of all the partner they are trying to help. Everything you have learned in this book runs on your own steadiness, and steadiness is not infinite.

What supporting can cost you

Let us be plain about the costs, because they are real and measurable and naming them is not disloyal. Research consistently finds that partners of people with post-traumatic stress carry more psychological distress than partners of people without it, including general distress, caregiver burden, and symptoms that echo trauma itself (Lambert et al., 2012). Caregiver burden is a specific thing, the accumulated weight of feeling that your health, your social life, or your peace of mind is being consumed by caring for someone (Beckham et al., 1996). It is not weakness. It is a predictable result of carrying a heavy load for a long time, and pretending you are not carrying it does not make it lighter.

There is a second cost with its own name, and knowing the name helps. Secondary traumatic stress, sometimes called compassion fatigue, describes how people who are close to a trauma survivor can begin to develop trauma-like responses of their own, absorbed through proximity and care (Figley, 1995). You may find yourself hypervigilant, easily startled, having intrusive thoughts about your partner's worst moments, feeling that the world has become less safe. The National Center for PTSD notes that partners can develop these responses simply from being close to someone else's trauma (National Center for PTSD, n.d.-a). If this is happening to you, you are not overreacting or being fragile. You are having a known response to a real exposure, and it deserves care rather than dismissal.

The Oxygen Order

The principle here is borrowed from the safety card in every airplane, and it is not a metaphor, it is a rule. Put your own oxygen mask on first, before you help the person next to you, because you cannot help anyone if you have passed out. Call it the Oxygen Order. It is not selfishness. It is sequence. A supporter who neglects their own needs until they collapse is not more devoted. They are heading for a collapse that will take the support down with them. Your wellbeing is not in competition with your partner's. It is the precondition for your being any use to them at all.

This reorders how you think about your own needs. Rest, friendship, your own interests, time away, your own mental health care, these are not indulgences you earn once your partner is stable. They are the oxygen that keeps you conscious enough to help. A partner who protects their sleep, keeps their friendships, holds onto their own life, and tends their own mind is not taking something away from the person they love. They are maintaining the only resource the support actually depends on, which is a supporter who has not burned to the ground.

The slow disappearance

The danger rarely arrives as a decision. It arrives as a slow disappearance, one reasonable sacrifice at a time, until you look up and find that your world has shrunk to a single room and a single person's states. Valenor, thirty-five, described it exactly this way. He had not chosen to stop seeing his brother, or to quit the running club, or to let his own therapy lapse. Each of those had fallen away for a sensible reason, a hard week, a bad night, a sense that he should be available. But the reasons had added up to a life in which he did nothing but monitor and manage, and he was so depleted that his patience, the very thing his partner needed most, had worn down to nothing.

Valenor's turning point was ugly, which is how these turning points usually are. He snapped, badly, over something small, and frightened both himself and his partner. What that snap revealed was not that he was a bad partner but that he was an empty one, running on fumes, with nothing left to give because he had given it all and refilled none of it. His recovery was not a matter of trying harder. It was a matter of putting things back, the brother, the running, the therapy, the small pieces of a self he had let dissolve. As he refilled, his patience returned, and the irony was not lost on him that the best thing he did for his partner that year was start doing things without her.

Resentment is information

The feeling partners are most ashamed of is resentment, and it is worth rescuing from shame, because resentment is not a character flaw. It is information. Resentment is what accumulates when you give past your limits for too long without replenishment. It is the psyche's way of reporting that the account is overdrawn. Treating resentment as evidence that you are a bad person is both untrue and useless, because it makes you hide the feeling rather than address its cause. The cause is almost always some version of the slow disappearance, too much given, too little kept, boundaries dissolved, self neglected.

The response to resentment is not to shame yourself out of it, which does not work, but to read it as the signal it is and act on the cause.

Where have you overextended? What have you given up that you need back? Which fence, in the language of Chapter 5, has quietly fallen? Resentment tends to shrink when the underlying depletion is addressed, and it tends to grow when it is ignored or suppressed. Self-compassion research suggests that treating your own struggle with the same kindness you would offer a friend is not indulgence but a resource that helps people stay functional under strain (Neff, 2003). Meeting your own resentment with curiosity rather than contempt is where its usefulness begins.

You need your own support

Here is a sentence to take seriously: you need support that is not your partner. This is not optional, and it is not a sign that your relationship has failed. You are carrying a real and heavy load, and no one should carry it alone or expect the person they are supporting to also be their sole source of comfort about the very difficulty they are living through. You need people, plural, and ideally at least one of them professional. A therapist of your own is not an admission of defeat. It is oxygen. Partners of trauma survivors benefit from their own independent support, and the absence of it is a reliable predictor of burning out (Nelson Goff & Smith, 2005).

Evanthe, forty, had told herself for two years that she did not need help, that her partner was the one with the problem, that seeking support for herself would be self-indulgent when her partner was suffering so much more. The isolation nearly ended the relationship. When she finally started seeing a therapist of her own and reconnected with two friends who knew what she was living, the change was not that her partner got easier. Her partner did not get easier. The change was that Evanthe stopped facing it alone, and facing it with support turned out to be a completely different experience from facing it in isolation, even when the facts of the situation were identical.

Cyrel refills the tank

Cyrel, whom you have followed and watched fail, was quietly running on empty by this point in his story, and it was part of why the night he left had gone so badly. His own depletion had left him with no reserve, so when the moment demanded more than he had, he grabbed his keys instead. As he and Éloane rebuilt after that night, Cyrel did something he had resisted for a long time. He went back to his own counseling, told two old friends the truth about what his life had become, and stopped treating his own needs as the last item on a list that never ended. It did not fix everything, and Éloane's trauma remained her own long road. But a Cyrel with something in the tank was a steadier partner than the empty one, and the difference showed in the moments that counted.

Not your job to regulate them

We return, one more time, to the belief that has haunted this whole book, because it is the engine of most supporter burnout. You are not responsible for regulating your partner's nervous system. You cannot do it, no matter how much you sacrifice, and the attempt is precisely what empties you. Their recovery is their own, ideally supported by their own professional care. Your role is to support, to steady, to hold your own boundaries, and to stay a whole person. It is not to be the manager of another adult's healing. Letting go of that impossible job is not abandoning your partner. It is releasing a weight you were never meant to carry and could not carry anyway, and it is often the single most freeing shift a supporting partner can make.

Two views, turned toward you

For eight chapters the two panels looked outward, at your partner. This chapter turns them around, because the person who most needs an honest, non-diagnosing witness right now may be you.

What may be happening for you. You may be carrying caregiver burden, the accumulated weight of feeling your health, your social life, and your peace of mind being consumed by the role, and mistaking it for personal weakness. You may be developing secondary traumatic stress, becoming hypervigilant, easily startled, braced for threat, having absorbed some of the trauma through proximity and care. You may be feeling a resentment you are ashamed of, without recognizing it as information about an overdrawn account rather than a flaw in your character. You may have disappeared into the role one reasonable sacrifice at a time, until your world shrank to a single room and a single person's states. And you may be running on the impossible belief that it is your job to regulate another adult's nervous system, a job that cannot be done and that empties you in the trying.

What you can do about it. You can name these costs honestly, treating burden and secondary stress as known responses to a real exposure rather than as evidence that you are failing. You can read your resentment as a signal and address its cause, restoring the fences and the pieces of yourself that have quietly dissolved. You can put your own oxygen mask on first, protecting your sleep, your friendships, your interests, and your own care as the precondition for helping at all. You can build support that is not your partner, ideally including a professional of your own, so that you are not facing this alone. And you can set down the job of regulating your partner, which was never yours and never possible, freeing the energy that impossible job consumed.

The device that helped you see your partner clearly works just as well turned inward. You are allowed to be an uncertain, compassionate witness to your own exhaustion, and doing so is not self-indulgence. It is maintenance of the one resource this entire book depends on.

This week

Your practice this week is to put one thing back. Identify one piece of your own life that has quietly disappeared, a friendship, an activity, an appointment with your own care, a small pleasure, and take one concrete step to restore it this week. Send the text. Book the session. Go for the run. It does not have to be large. It has to be yours, something that refills you rather than something you do for your partner. Notice, if you can, the guilt that comes with it, and do the thing anyway, because that guilt is the exact voice that shrank your world in the first place. One restored piece is the beginning of putting your own mask on.

A question partners ask

Partners often ask how they are supposed to justify spending time or money on their own care when their partner is the one who is suffering, and the resources feel like they should go to the person with the diagnosis. The reframe is that your care is not competing with your partner's, it is underwriting it, because the support your partner receives from you is only as steady as the person providing it. A depleted supporter is not a generous one, whatever their intentions, and the collapse that neglect leads to costs the relationship far more than an hour of therapy or an evening with friends ever would. Spending on your own steadiness is spending on the relationship, not against it. The guilt that says otherwise is the same voice that shrank your world one sacrifice at a time, and it is not a reliable guide. Treat your own oxygen as a shared resource, because it is one. The steadier you are, the more your partner actually has to lean on.

Your Own Oxygen

I want to leave you with the reason this matters beyond your own survival, because supporters are often more willing to act for their partner's sake than their own. Your oxygen is not only yours. When you are rested, connected, supported, and still a whole person, you bring a steadiness to the relationship that no technique in this book can substitute for. The calm presence that helps in a flashback comes from a nervous system that is not itself depleted. The patience, the fewer words, the kind fence, the steady return, all of it runs on a supporter who has not run dry. Protecting yourself is how you protect the thing you are trying to protect. And there is one more thing you must protect above all others, one line that no amount of love or trauma or devotion should ever move, and that line is the subject of the final chapter.

Chapter 10: When It Is Not a Flashback

Lioren, thirty-six, had spent three years explaining her partner's behavior to herself. The controlling of the money was because of his trauma. The tracking of where she went was because his history made him anxious. The names he called her during his worst moments were the flashback talking, not him. The time he blocked the door so she could not leave a fight was, she told herself, a freeze response, a symptom, something to be met with compassion. She had read about trauma. She had learned to be an uncertain witness, to use fewer words, to hold the two truths. And she had used every one of those good skills to explain away a pattern that was not a flashback at all.

This chapter exists because the skills in this book can be turned against you, and a book that taught them without teaching this would be dangerous. Everything you have learned assumes a certain kind of situation, a partner whose trauma sometimes floods them in ways that are hard but not designed to control or harm you. There is a different situation that can wear the same clothing, and telling them apart is the most important discernment a supporting partner ever makes. It is also the one that trauma knowledge, wrongly applied, makes harder, because every tool for extending compassion can become a tool for excusing the inexcusable.

Two things that must both be true

I have to hold two truths in this chapter that some readers will want to pull apart, and I will not let them be pulled apart, because separating them causes harm in both directions. The first truth is that most people with post-traumatic stress are not violent, and the fear that they are is a stigma that keeps people from seeking help and paints millions of struggling people as dangerous when they are not (Elbogen & Johnson, 2009; Taft et al., 2011). The second truth is that a trauma history never, under any circumstances, obligates you to remain in a situation that endangers you. Both are true. Holding only the first leads you to excuse harm. Holding only the second leads you to fear a whole population of people who deserve compassion. The discernment lives in holding both.

The research bears out the need for care in both directions. Post-traumatic stress is associated, at a population level, with more relationship conflict and, in some studies, with a higher likelihood of aggression, and it is also true that most individuals with it are never aggressive at all (Taft et al., 2011; National Center for PTSD, n.d.-b). These facts are not in conflict. They mean that trauma raises the importance of watching honestly, not that trauma predicts danger in any given person. Your job is not to decide what people with trauma are like in general. Your job is to see clearly what is happening in your own home, without either the reflex to excuse or the reflex to fear.

The Bright Line

The principle of this chapter is the firmest one in the book, and it does not bend. Trauma explains behavior. It never requires you to stay in danger. Call it the Bright Line. On one side of the line is the whole world of hard, painful, exhausting, non-dangerous difficulty that the rest of this book addresses, the flashbacks and the harsh words and the shut-downs and the circular fights. On the other side of the line is behavior that threatens your physical safety, controls and isolates you, or makes you genuinely afraid, and on that side of the line the tools of this book do not apply, because you are no longer in the situation those tools were made for. The Bright Line is not a suggestion. It is the floor beneath everything.

What makes the Bright Line hard is that a person in a genuinely controlling or abusive relationship is often the last to see it, precisely because they are compassionate, because they understand trauma, because they have been taught that love means patience. Those good qualities become the very things that keep them explaining away a pattern that a stranger would name in a moment. This is why the line has to be stated as a rule rather than a feeling, because the feeling, in these situations, has usually been trained to look the wrong way. If you find yourself using your trauma knowledge to explain why you should tolerate fear, that use of the knowledge is itself a warning sign.

How to tell the difference

There are honest distinctions between a flashback and something that crosses the line, and it helps to name them, though no list replaces your own clear seeing. A flashback is a state that comes and goes, that your partner does not want, that they feel remorse about afterward, and that is not aimed at controlling you. A pattern of abuse or control is directed, persistent, and serves a function, which is power over you, and it tends to follow a logic even when it is dressed as symptom. Freeze responses do not conveniently block the exit only during arguments the person is losing. Flashbacks do not selectively target your bank account, your friendships, and your freedom of movement. When the behavior consistently serves control, the trauma frame is being used as cover, whether or not real trauma also exists.

Another distinction is what happens over time and after the fact. A partner whose hard moments are flashbacks generally wants to do better, participates in repair when they can, and does not require you to shrink your life to avoid their anger. A partner whose behavior crosses the line tends to make you responsible for their moods, to escalate when you set boundaries, and to leave you more afraid and smaller over time rather than steadier. The single most useful question is not what is happening inside my partner, which you cannot fully know, but what is happening to me. Am I becoming more myself in this relationship, or less. Am I safer over time, or more afraid. Those questions cut through the explanations.

Fear is data

If there is one instrument to trust in this chapter, it is fear, your own, of the specific kind that is about your body and your safety. Not the ordinary fear of a hard conversation, but the fear that makes you calculate where the exits are, that makes you manage your partner to prevent an explosion, that makes you afraid of what will happen if you say the wrong thing. That fear is data, and trauma knowledge should never be used to talk yourself out of it. Herman, whose work helped define our understanding of trauma, wrote about how the conditions of ongoing danger reshape a person's perceptions and can teach them to doubt their own alarm (Herman, 1992). If your own safety-fear has gone quiet through long training, its return is worth listening to, not overriding.

Lioren's turning point came when a friend asked her a simple question that her trauma knowledge had not let her ask herself: are you afraid of him. She started to explain the trauma, the history, the symptoms, and then she stopped, because underneath all the explanation the answer was yes. She had been afraid for a long time, and she had used everything she knew about compassion to avoid the word. Naming the fear did not resolve her situation, which was complicated and took time and outside help to address safely. But it moved her from explaining to seeing, and the seeing was the thing that had been missing.

When you are not sure

Many situations are not as clear as Lioren's, and I will not pretend the line is always obvious in the moment. Sometimes you genuinely cannot tell whether what you are living is hard-but-safe or something that crosses the line, and the uncertainty itself is exhausting. When you are not sure, the move is not to decide alone, because the isolation of these situations is exactly what clouds judgment. The move is to bring in an outside perspective, someone whose view is not shaped by the daily fog, whether that is a trusted friend, your own therapist, or a professional who specializes in these situations. Sorell, forty-five, spent a year unsure whether his partner's rages were flashbacks or something more, and what finally clarified it was not more solitary analysis but a counselor of his own who could see what he had grown too close to see.

Getting outside input is not disloyal, and it is not a betrayal of your partner's privacy or their trauma. It is what people do when they are too close to a situation to judge it, which is a normal human limit, not a failure. A partner whose behavior is genuinely non-dangerous has nothing to fear from you talking to a therapist about your relationship. A situation that cannot survive you getting an outside perspective is itself telling you something. If your partner reacts to the idea of you having support of your own with escalation or threats, that reaction is information about which side of the line you are on.

If you are in danger

I need to speak plainly for a moment, because some readers of this book are in real danger, and gentleness would fail them. If your partner has hurt you physically, threatened your safety, or made you afraid for your body, that is not a flashback to be met with the tools in this book, and your safety comes before everything, including your compassion, your relationship, and your understanding of their trauma. You do not owe anyone your endangerment, and no history, however genuine, changes that. If you are in immediate danger, contact your local emergency services. If you need help thinking through a frightening situation, domestic violence hotlines and local services exist for exactly this, and reaching one does not commit you to any particular decision. It gives you information and options from people who understand these situations well.

I am not able to promise you how any particular service will handle your specific circumstances, because that varies, and you deserve honesty rather than false assurance. What I can tell you is that you do not have to figure out the dangerous situations alone, that the compassion you have extended to your partner is also owed to yourself, and that leaving a situation that endangers you is not a failure of love or loyalty. It is the most basic form of self-respect, and it is allowed, always, without permission from anyone.

Two views, held with care

The two panels return one last time, but in this chapter they carry a warning as much as a guide, because the panel about your partner is exactly the one that can be misused to keep you in danger. Read the second panel as the one that governs when the two disagree.

What may be happening for your partner. In the hard-but-safe world this book mostly addresses, their difficult moments may be states they do not want, feel remorse about, and do not aim at controlling you, states that come and go rather than serving a steady function. But you cannot fully know their inner experience, and this is precisely the limit that must not be used against you. A trauma frame may be genuinely true and still be doing work it should not do, if it is being used, by them or by you, to explain away a pattern that consistently serves power over you. The inner column, in other words, is the one you can least verify and should least rely on when your own safety is the question.

What you can do about it, and what governs when they conflict. You can shift the question from what is happening inside my partner, which you cannot know, to what is happening to me, which you can. You can watch whether you are becoming more yourself in this relationship or less, safer over time or more afraid. You can treat your safety-fear, the kind about your body and the exits, as data rather than something to talk yourself out of with trauma knowledge. You can refuse to decide alone, bringing in an outside perspective that is not caught in the daily fog. And you can hold the Bright Line as a rule rather than a feeling, because in these situations the feeling has often been trained to look the wrong way. When the first panel and the second conflict, the second wins, always, because your safety is not a matter of interpretation.

That inversion is the whole point of this chapter. Everywhere else in the book, the humble uncertainty of the first panel is a virtue. Here, it is the thing most likely to be turned against you, and so here, and only here, the outer view of your own safety overrides the inner guess about your partner every time.

This is a heavy chapter

This has been a hard chapter to read, and if it stirred something uncomfortable, that discomfort may be worth paying attention to rather than pushing away. Most readers of this book are in the hard-but-safe world the rest of it addresses, and for them this chapter is a boundary marker they will rarely need to approach. Some readers are closer to the line than they have let themselves know, and for them this chapter is the most important one, and the discomfort it raised is a signal to talk to someone outside the fog. If that is you, please consider reaching out to a trusted person or a professional, not because anything is certainly wrong, but because a clear outside view is exactly what these situations require and exactly what they make hard to get.

A question partners ask

Partners in genuinely uncertain situations often ask how they can act on the Bright Line when they are not even sure the line has been crossed, when everything is murky and they fear overreacting as much as underreacting. The answer is that you do not have to be certain to seek an outside perspective, and seeking one is not an accusation. Talking honestly with your own therapist, a trusted person, or a service that understands these situations is a reasonable response to uncertainty itself, not a verdict you are passing on your partner. Clarity, in these situations, rarely comes from more solitary analysis, because isolation is exactly what clouds judgment. It comes from letting someone outside the daily fog reflect back what they see. You are allowed to get help thinking, before you are anywhere near a decision, and doing so commits you to nothing. If uncertainty itself has become a heavy, ongoing weight, that weight is reason enough to bring another set of eyes to your situation, gently and without waiting for proof.

The Line That Protects Both of You

Let me end by reframing the Bright Line as what it actually is, which is not a wall against your partner but a protection for both of you. A relationship in which your safety is never at risk is a better relationship for your partner too, because it is honest, because it does not ask you to erase yourself, and because it does not let a trauma frame quietly excuse harm that harms the person doing it as much as the person receiving it. Holding the line does not stigmatize the many people with trauma who are never dangerous. It honors them, by refusing to let the rare exceptions hide behind the same word. And it honors you, by insisting that your safety is not negotiable and never was. That is where a partner's field guide has to end, not with a technique, but with a line, drawn clearly, that says compassion has a floor, and the floor is that you get to be safe. Everything else in this book is built on standing there.

Getting Support

Supporting a partner through trauma is not something anyone should do entirely alone, and reaching for help is a sign of steadiness, not weakness. If you are looking for support of your own, a few kinds are worth knowing about, and none of them commits you to any particular decision about your relationship.

For your own mental health, a licensed therapist or counselor can give you a place to process the weight you are carrying, ideally one with some understanding of trauma-affected relationships. You do not need to be in crisis to benefit, and having your own support is one of the most protective things a supporting partner can do.

If you or your partner are in crisis, or if you are having thoughts of harming yourself, contact your local emergency number or a crisis line in your country. In the United States, the 988 Suicide and Crisis Lifeline can be reached by calling or texting 988. Services and their procedures vary by country and by situation, so it is worth finding the specific resources available where you live before you need them.

If you are afraid for your physical safety, or if the patterns described in Chapter 10 sound like your situation, domestic violence services exist to help you think through frightening circumstances with people who understand them. In the United States, the National Domestic Violence Hotline can be reached at 1-800-799-7233. Reaching a service like this does not obligate you to make any particular choice. It gives you information and options.

For understanding your partner's experience, reputable organizations publish accessible, evidence-based information. The National Center for PTSD (ptsd.va.gov) offers material for families and partners, and national mental health bodies in most countries publish similar resources. Reading from established, professional sources is a good way to keep your understanding grounded.

References

Beckham, J. C., Lytle, B. L., & Feldman, M. E. (1996). Caregiver burden in partners of Vietnam War veterans with posttraumatic stress disorder. *Journal of Consulting and Clinical Psychology, 64*(5), 1068-1072. https://doi.org/10.1037/0022-006X.64.5.1068

Brewin, C. R., Dalgleish, T., & Joseph, S. (1996). A dual representation theory of posttraumatic stress disorder. *Psychological Review, 103*(4), 670-686. https://doi.org/10.1037/0033-295X.103.4.670

Cloitre, M., Shevlin, M., Brewin, C. R., Bisson, J. I., Roberts, N. P., Maercker, A., Karatzias, T., & Hyland, P. (2018). The International Trauma Questionnaire: Development of a self-report measure of ICD-11 PTSD and complex PTSD. *Acta Psychiatrica Scandinavica, 138*(6), 536-546. https://doi.org/10.1111/acps.12956

Ehlers, A., & Clark, D. M. (2000). A cognitive model of posttraumatic stress disorder. *Behaviour Research and Therapy, 38*(4), 319-345. https://doi.org/10.1016/S0005-7967(99)00123-0

Elbogen, E. B., & Johnson, S. C. (2009). The intricate link between violence and mental disorder: Results from the National Epidemiologic Survey on Alcohol and Related Conditions. *Archives of General Psychiatry, 66*(2), 152–161. https://doi.org/10.1001/archgenpsychiatry.2008.537

Figley, C. R. (Ed.). (1995). *Compassion fatigue: Coping with secondary traumatic stress disorder in those who treat the traumatized.* Brunner/Mazel.

Fredman, S. J., Vorstenbosch, V., Wagner, A. C., Macdonald, A., & Monson, C. M. (2014). Partner accommodation in posttraumatic stress disorder: Initial testing of the Significant Others' Responses to Trauma Scale (SORTS). *Journal of Anxiety Disorders, 28*(4), 372-381. https://doi.org/10.1016/j.janxdis.2014.04.001

Gottman, J. M., & Silver, N. (1999). *The seven principles for making marriage work.* Crown.

Herman, J. L. (1992). *Trauma and recovery: The aftermath of violence.* Basic Books.

Karatzias, T., Murphy, P., Cloitre, M., Bisson, J., Roberts, N., Shevlin, M., Hyland, P., Maercker, A., Ben-Ezra, M., Coventry, P., Mason-Roberts, S., Bradley, A., & Hutton, P. (2019). Psychological interventions for ICD-11 complex PTSD symptoms: Systematic review and meta-analysis. *Psychological Medicine, 49*(11), 1761-1775. https://doi.org/10.1017/S0033291719000436

Kessler, R. C. (2000). Posttraumatic stress disorder: The burden to the individual and to society. *Journal of Clinical Psychiatry, 61*(Suppl 5), 4-12.

Lambert, J. E., Engh, R., Hasbun, A., & Holzer, J. (2012). Impact of posttraumatic stress disorder on the relationship quality and psychological distress of intimate partners: A meta-analytic review. *Journal of Family Psychology, 26*(5), 729-737. https://doi.org/10.1037/a0029341

LeDoux, J. E. (1996). *The emotional brain: The mysterious underpinnings of emotional life.* Simon & Schuster.

Monson, C. M., & Fredman, S. J. (2012). *Cognitive-behavioral conjoint therapy for PTSD: Harnessing the healing power of relationships.* Guilford Press.

National Center for PTSD. (n.d.-a). *PTSD and the family.* U.S. Department of Veterans Affairs. https://www.ptsd.va.gov/professional/treat/specific/ptsd_family.asp

National Center for PTSD. (n.d.-b). *Anger and trauma.* U.S. Department of Veterans Affairs. https://www.ptsd.va.gov/understand/related/anger.asp

Neff, K. D. (2003). The development and validation of a scale to measure self-compassion. *Self and Identity, 2*(3), 223-250. https://doi.org/10.1080/15298860309027

Nelson Goff, B. S., & Smith, D. B. (2005). Systemic traumatic stress: The couple adaptation to traumatic stress model. *Journal of Marital and Family Therapy, 31*(2), 145-157. https://doi.org/10.1111/j.1752-0606.2005.tb01552.x

Ogden, P., Minton, K., & Pain, C. (2006). *Trauma and the body: A sensorimotor approach to psychotherapy.* W. W. Norton.

Renshaw, K. D., Rodrigues, C. S., & Jones, D. H. (2008). Psychological symptoms and marital satisfaction in spouses of Operation Iraqi Freedom veterans: Relationships with spouses' perceptions of veterans' experiences and symptoms. *Journal of Family Psychology, 22*(4), 586-594. https://doi.org/10.1037/0893-3200.22.3.586

Siegel, D. J. (1999). *The developing mind: How relationships and the brain interact to shape who we are.* Guilford Press.

Taft, C. T., Watkins, L. E., Stafford, J., Street, A. E., & Monson, C. M. (2011). Posttraumatic stress disorder and intimate relationship problems: A meta-analysis. *Journal of Consulting and Clinical Psychology, 79*(1), 22-33. https://doi.org/10.1037/a0022196

van der Kolk, B. A. (2014). *The body keeps the score: Brain, mind, and body in the healing of trauma.* Viking.

Walker, P. (2013). *Complex PTSD: From surviving to thriving: A guide and map for recovering from childhood trauma.* Azure Coyote.